Resistance of the Sensible World

John D. Caputo, *series editor*

PERSPECTIVES IN
CONTINENTAL
PHILOSOPHY

EMMANUEL ALLOA

Resistance of the Sensible World
An Introduction to Merleau-Ponty

TRANSLATED BY JANE MARIE TODD

FORDHAM UNIVERSITY PRESS
New York ∎ 2017

This volume was originally published in French as *La résistance du sensible. Merleau-Ponty critique de la transparence*, © Éditions Kimé, Paris, 2008.

Cet ouvrage publié dans le cadre du programme d'aide à la publication bénéficie du soutien du Ministère des Affaires Etrangères et du Service Culturel de l'Ambassade de France représenté aux Etats-Unis.

This work received support from the French Ministry of Foreign Affairs and the Cultural Services of the French Embassy in the United States through their publishing assistance program.

Fordham University Press has no responsibility for the persistence or accuracy of URLs for external or third-party Internet websites referred to in this publication and does not guarantee that any content on such websites is, or will remain, accurate or appropriate.

Fordham University Press also publishes its books in a variety of electronic formats. Some content that appears in print may not be available in electronic books.

Visit us online at www.fordhampress.com.

Library of Congress Cataloging-in-Publication Data available online at http://catalog.loc.gov.

Printed and bound in Great Britain by
Marston Book Services Ltd, Oxfordshire

19 18 17   5 4 3 2 1

First edition

Contents

Foreword

The era when the evocation of Maurice Merleau-Ponty's phenomenology met with the silence of ignorance or rejection seems very far away and is, in fact, gone forever. It is an understatement to say that the philosopher has been "rediscovered," since, with rare exceptions, no one had really read him. In actuality, in less than two decades Merleau-Ponty has gone from the status of a minor or marginal author to that of a classic philosopher, so much so that the risk faced by the unusually large number of commentators is that of displaying overreverence or simply of producing an academic gloss. The elation of the early days, marked by the discovery of the enormous descriptive and critical potentialities of Merleau-Ponty's oeuvre, has given way to systematic, scholarly research, fueled by the assimilation of the many unpublished writings, attentive to the multiplicity of sources and the complexity of the development of Merleau-Ponty's writings as a whole. Increasingly, the difficult things are to resist the temptation to embalm him, a move absolutely at odds with the very meaning of Merleau-Ponty's enterprise, and to resist being crushed by the mass of commentary; in short, the difficult thing is to continue to see Merleau-Ponty's works with new eyes, those with which, according to Merleau-Ponty himself, the painter sees the world.

Emmanuel Alloa is among those who have averted the risks. He is familiar with and in command of the critical literature and the theoretical context in which Merleau-Ponty's thought took shape. And yet he reads him as if for the first time, as if nothing of what has been repeated again and again could be taken for granted. The condition that governs such a way of looking is both a great distance and a great proximity. On the one hand, Alloa considers matters from high above and far away; that is, he situates Merleau-Ponty within a long history of thought and thus links his phenomenology to problems that were already those of the Greek philosophers. The result is a relativization both historical and theoretical, one that can shed new light on Merleau-Ponty's oeuvre. On the other hand, that distance taken toward Merleau-Ponty's thought, which situates the issues in their broader theoretical context, eventually turns into a great proximity to the letter of the text. Alloa is attentive to the recurrence of certain words that have heretofore gone almost unnoticed and on which he confers the status of concepts (at least operative ones), while bringing to light all their semantic and historical implications. Like Merleau-Ponty's perceived thing, the word must come with all its roots and associations, and with the theoretical uses that have become sedimented within it. It is on that condition that it can cease to be self-evident, can break off from the flow of the text and become one of the prisms through which thought is refracted.

That is the status that Alloa confers on *transparency,* which is at first sight a simple term, sometimes a metaphor, but one that has a strong presence in Merleau-Ponty's writings, so much so that one is justified in seeing it as a secret driving force and central motif, on the basis of which a new coherence of the oeuvre may be constituted. It is, of course, a negative motif: Merleau-Ponty, aware as he was of the weight of the assumption of transparency in the history of thought—which is only the stronger for having most often remained hidden—sets out to establish through and through a *"critique of any ideology of transparency,* whether it be the self's transparency to itself, the transparency of knowledge to the self, or the transparency to the self of others" (see the introduction). It is this incessant struggle against the ideology of transparency, which is also a struggle between Merleau-Ponty and himself, that Alloa depicts in this book. The question naturally arises: What is the positive side of that critique? What can be placed in opposition to transparency? Attentive to the indisputable influence of Gaston Bachelard's phenomenology on Merleau-Ponty, Alloa, in an allusion to Jean Starobinski, posits as its contrary "the obstacle." Merleau-Ponty's philosophy, because it is a mode of thought that seeks to escape the ideology of transparency, is a philosophy of resistance or adversity. Because resistance is first and foremost resistance to language and thought, his philosophy enfolds a reflection on its own language, which is to say, ultimately, on its very possibility. Nevertheless, Alloa does not let the matter rest with that term, which he evokes seemingly in passing and which stands as the formulation of the problem rather than its solution. The question, in fact, is what precise form that irreducible coefficient of resistance of the real takes. How to name what makes the horizon of transparency forever unrealizable? Alloa's book is an attempt to elaborate figures of resistance, to identify and make explicit the terms or concepts on which the rejection of transparency has its foundation and becomes legible.

The first phase of Merleau-Ponty's oeuvre, which ends with *Phenomenology of Perception,* is centered on the notion of the body. The discovery of the embodiment constitutive of the subject allows Merleau-Ponty to move beyond all the idealist and intellectualist versions of perception and thereby to bring to light the essential inscription of sense in the sensible. Alloa, for his part, foregrounds the notion of *milieu,* recalling its rich history, and thus seizes on the body from the standpoint of its relation to an *Umwelt.* Indeed, according to Merleau-Ponty, "For a living being, having a body means being united with a definite milieu, merging with certain projects, and being perpetually engaged therein" (*PP,* 97/84). In understanding one's own body as belonging essentially to a milieu and as acting within it, as a *"potentiality in a milieu"* (see chapter 1 in the section titled "From the Milieu to the World"), one provides oneself with the means to preserve its specificity: The body cannot be reduced to a pure subject, nor does it submit fully to the laws of nature. That approach to the body allows Alloa to establish an enlightening contrast: He rightly takes issue with the idea that Merleau-Ponty's notion of the world can be derived from that of Heidegger. The animal's relation to the *Umwelt* cannot be thought in terms of encirclement (*Eingenommensein*) or captivation (*Benommenheit*), as Heidegger claims, but rather, consistent with the lesson of Kurt Goldstein, as a debate or clash of forces (*Auseinandersetzung*). For Heidegger, the milieu is a place of closure and encirclement; for Merleau-Ponty, it is synonymous with openness. Alloa is therefore right to conclude that, though both human beings and animals are fundamentally *"situated in* a milieu and *open to* it, . . . human beings potentiate that openness by creating their own worlds" (chapter 1 in the section titled "From the Milieu to the World"). In other words, the body is essentially *mediation.* It is the milieu of the milieu (the world), in two senses: It is both its center or "middle" (*milieu* in French) and its "medium." It is not surprising that, in the later Merleau-Ponty, the focus shifts from mediated beings to mediation itself. This milieu of the body— at once the heart of the world and the vector of its appearing—which will henceforth be called flesh, delivers the true sense of being of that first milieu, the world. Alloa skillfully shows that the import of the notion of milieu extends far beyond the use made of it in *Phenomenology of Perception:* It designates what must be thought in lieu of an "epistemology of transparency."

The notions of "massive reality" or "envelope phenomenon," set in motion in the lecture courses on *Nature*, are therefore only reformulations of it.

Alloa then turns to the question of language. He thus follows an order that, according to all the commentators, is that of Merleau-Ponty's oeuvre itself. In reality, however, the reflection on transparency provides an even better justification for the necessity of that order. In fact, what is characteristic of speech, at least as it usually functions, is that it forgets it is a fact, an event, that it is beholden to a material sound, and appears to itself as the pure expression of an ideality that would precede speech itself and owe nothing to it. Language conceals itself or effaces itself by its very operation: It institutes a transparency, which is at once and necessarily a transparency of the material sound to meaning (meaning passes through it), a transparency of the meaning itself, and, as a result, of that meaning to thought. To say that meaning is transparent is to acknowledge that it shines through [*transparaît*] fully in the material, wholly effacing it and, consequently, that it gives itself to thought in a transparent manner, in such a way, that is, as to offer it no resistance, so that a perfect adequation becomes realizable. It is therefore not surprising that a philosophy that wants to be done with "the ideology of transparency" should confront at length the question of language, inasmuch as the effectiveness of language lies in an act of speech within which the material sound brings about its own effacement. Hence the necessity of engaging in a sort of "reduction" of speech, which no longer entails approaching it from the transparent sphere of meaning or from an opaque matter—which is only the necessary counterpoint to that meaning—but on the basis of the movement leading from one to the other and, in reality, deeper than both. To anyone who *examines* the movement of signification rather than being swept up in it, it appears clear that the very categories on the basis of which that movement in general is described, including in *Phenomenology of Perception,* must be abandoned: The phenomenology of speech issues a challenge to the philosophy of transparency, even in its least obvious forms, and that is why such a phenomenology moves beyond itself toward an ontology of a new kind. Alloa skillfully shows that Merleau-Ponty, in centering his inquiry on the "transparent body of language," is not content simply to redirect what he had established in his prior studies of the body, that is, to insert meaning into a living body by making speech one gesture among others. On the contrary, in light of Saussurean linguistics, he is led to revise his conception of the living body and to conceive of it as a diacritical system (chapter 2 in the section titled "The Diacritical").

Nevertheless, as Merleau-Ponty reminds us, "Any inquiry into the philosophy of language presupposes an inquiry into the language of philosophy" (chapter 2 in the section titled "From the Literal to the Lateral"). In other words, that detour through linguistics and the phenomenology of speech does not leave intact the meaning Merleau-Ponty confers on philosophy and, consequently, on its "object." The ontology Merleau-Ponty was hoping for coincides with the inauguration of a new philosophical style, which Mikel Dufrenne felicitously calls "philosophizing without philosophemes." The orientation of the later Merleau-Ponty indisputably proceeds from a concern to transfer the insights gained about the phenomenology of language to the level of perception, that is, to move toward a common source of perceptual sense and linguistic sense.

The aim of the third stage in Merleau-Ponty's thought "was to excavate the common ground between the 1945 book and the investigations of language, to reconstitute the fabric, its weft and warp, on which something can be given to me as visible and through which words can give an account of it" (chapter 3 in the section titled "Thinking according to the Image"). It is obviously within that perspective that one must understand Merleau-Ponty's reflections on painting, about which Alloa goes so far as to say that they "definitively cast off the outer hull of classic aesthetics," to move "from a philosophy of painting to a philosophy *after* painting (in the sense that a painter who imitates Cézanne's style paints "after" Cézanne) or—more exactly—a philosophy *according to* painting, of which *Eye and Mind* would be the first draft" (chapter 3 in the section titled "Thinking according to the Image"). In any event, the inquiry into the origin or root of meaning, in terms of its neutrality vis-à-vis the distinction between the visible and the sayable, gives rise to an ontology of the flesh or of wild being. That ontology can be understood as a radicalization of the notion of milieu. If the body can be "a 'means' in a world-milieu" (chapter 3 in the section titled "The Styles of the World"), it is because that body is more than a means: It is made of the same stuff as the world it mediatizes, and the concept of milieu must therefore be understood as referring to an element common to the body and the world, to their originary kinship. The concept in question is that of a "formative milieu" of the subject and the object, the essence and the fact, the body and the world. Alloa felicitously follows a number of motifs of that ontology of the flesh by closely examining the concept of chiasm, which has been endlessly rehashed but rarely considered head on. This part of his book includes a number of insights that are extremely helpful: for example, the demonstration of Derrida's error concerning the chiasm of touching/touched, which he understood as the final stage of a philosophy of presence, whereas in reality it is the exordium to a philosophy of nonpresence and nontransparency, the definition of flesh as the "embodied diacritical" (chapter 3 in the section titled "Ontology of the Flesh").

Alloa goes even further. He shows that despite all the methodological dilemmas that the later Merleau-Ponty is caught in, various systematic breakthroughs can be identified, such as a renewed theory of essences, which reformulates Husserl's problem of eidetic reduction, or such as a thoroughly revised theory of the universal. Yet it seems as if Merleau-Ponty was caught in insurmountable dichotomies, which an opposition such as that between the *visible and the invisible* bespeaks. Alloa patiently collects the hints toward another, alternative approach, which consists in reconsidering the "medium" of visibility. That path, which would allow us to confront the question of the essence of visibility, the central question of Merleau-Ponty's posthumous writings, would entail taking the full measure of the fact that vision excludes adequation and, on the contrary, implies a distance that is not an obstacle to knowledge but its guarantee, a distance that is therefore not a distance *between* the one seeing and the visible—the flip side of proximity—but, precisely, the fabric that connects them. Alloa reads the extraordinary and enigmatic text from *Eye and Mind* about the bottom of a swimming pool, which I see not *despite* the water and its reflections but *through* them, as a sample of what that third way might be. It is a philosophy of the *diaphanous*, as Alloa calls it, taking that notion from Aristotle—the being of the "between," an element that allows something "that belongs to the visible without being visible in actuality to shine through" (conclusion)—in which the thinking of the milieu as *medium* would be achieved and would lead to a philosophy of trans-lucidity or of trans-appearing, which the author also calls "dia-phenomenology." These stimulating and promising propositions open the way for many further investigations and in themselves provide a reason to read this original and inspired book.

Renaud Barbaras

Translator's Note

References to Merleau-Ponty's writings appear in the body of the text. The French page number is given first, followed by the page number in the English-language translation, when available. Quotations are taken from the published translations, modified when necessary. See the list of abbreviations following this note. The corresponding English-language text is listed after the French version.

Abbreviations of Merleau-Ponty's Works

All works listed here are by Maurice Merleau-Ponty. In the text, references are given within parentheses by abbreviation followed by the page number to the French edition, followed by a virgule and the page number to the English translation, when there is one.

C   *Causeries, 1948.* Edited with notes by Stéphanie Ménasé. Paris: Seuil, 2002. [*The World of Perception.* Translated by Oliver Davis. London: Routledge, 2004.] Transcripts of a radio lecture series.

DE   *Douze entretiens avec Maurice Merleau-Ponty.* Recorded by Georges Chardonnier for Radiodiffusion-Télévision Française between May 25 and August 7, 1959. Archives de l'Institut National de l'Audiovisuel.

EP   *Éloge de la philosophie et autres essais.* Paris: Gallimard, 1953. [*In Praise of Philosophy and Other Essays.* Translated by John Wild and James Edie. Evanston, Ill.: Northwestern University Press, 1988.]

HCR   *Husserl: Troisième colloque philosophique de Royaumont.* Comments, pp. 157–59. Paris: Minuit, 1959. Proceedings of the colloquium held April 23–30, 1957.

IP   *L'institution-La passivité: Notes de cours au Collège de France (1954–1955).* Paris: Éditions Belin, 2003. [*Institution and Passivity: Course Notes from the Collège de France (1954–1955).*

Foreword by Claude Lefort. Translated by Leonard Lawlor and Heath Massey. Evanston, Ill.: Northwestern University Press, 2010.]

MBN   Manuscrits, Bibliothèque nationale. [Unpublished manuscripts from the Bibliothèque Nationale, Paris. Merleau-Ponty Collection]. Followed by volume number.

MPR   *The Merleau-Ponty Reader*, Edited by Ted Toadvine and Leonard Lawlor. Evanston, Ill.: Northwestern University Press, 2007.

MSME   *Le monde sensible et le monde de l'expression: Cours au Collège de France. Notes, 1953*. Text edited with notes by Emmanuel de Saint Aubert and Stefan Kristensen. Foreword by Emmanuel de Saint Aubert. Geneva: MētisPresses, 2011.

N   *La nature: Notes de cours du Collège de France*. Edited with notes by Dominique Séglard. Paris: Seuil, 1995. [*Nature: Course Notes from the Collège de France*. Edited with notes by Dominique Séglard. Translated by Robert Vallier. Evanston, Ill.: Northwestern University Press, 2003.]

NC   *Notes de cours au Collège de France 1958–1959 et 1960–1961*. Edited by Stéphanie Ménasé with a preface by Claude Lefort. Paris: Gallimard, 1996.

OE   *L'oeil et l'esprit*. Paris: Gallimard, 1964. [*Eye and Mind*, translated by Carleton Dallery, in *The Primacy of Perception and Other Essays on Phenomenological Psychology, the Philosophy of Art, History, and Politics*, 159–90. Evanston, Ill.: Northwestern University Press, 1964.]

OG   *Notes de cours sur* L'origine *de la géométrie* de Husserl, followed by *Recherches sur la phénoménologie de Merleau-Ponty*, edited by Renaud Barbaras. Paris: Presses Universitaires de France, 1998.

P1   *Parcours 1935–1951*. Edited by Jacques Prunair. Lagrasse: Verdier, 1997.

P2   *Parcours deux, 1951–1961*. Edited by Jacques Prunair. Lagrasse: Verdier, 2000.

PACR   *La philosophie analytique: Quatrième colloque de Royaumont*, response to Gilbert Ryle, 93–96. Paris: Minuit, 1962. ["Phenomenology and Analytic Philosophy," translated by James Hatley, in *Text and Dialogues: On Philosophy, Politics and Culture*, edited and with an introduction by Hugh J. Silverman and James Barry Jr., translated by Michael B.

	Smith et al., 59–71. Atlantic Highlands, N.J.: Humanities Press, 1992].
PM	*La prose du monde.* Edited with an introduction by Claude Lefort. Paris: Gallimard, 1969. [*The Prose of the World.* Edited by Claude Lefort. Translated by John O'Neill. Evanston, Ill.: Northwestern University Press, 1973.]
PP	*La phénoménologie de la perception.* Paris: Gallimard, 1945. [*Phenomenology of Perception.* Translated by Donald A. Landes. London: Routledge, 2012.]
PPE	*Psychologie et pédagogie de l'enfant: Cours de Sorbonne, 1949–1952.* Lagrasse: Verdier, 2001. [*Child Psychology and Pedagogy: The Sorbonne Lectures, 1949–1952.* Edited by James M. Edie, Anthony J. Steinbock, and John McCumber. Translated by Talia Welsh. Evanston, Ill.: Northwestern University Press, 2010.]
PrP	*Le primat de la perception et ses conséquences philosophiques.* ["The Primacy of Perception and Its Philosophical Consequences," translated by James M. Edie, in *The Primacy of Perception and Other Essays on Phenomenological Psychology, the Philosophy of Art, History, and Politics,* 12–42. Evanston, Ill.: Northwestern University Press, 1964]. Preceded by *Projet de travail sur la nature de la perception* (1933) and *La Nature de la perception* (1934) ["The Nature of Perception: Two Proposals," translated by Forrest W. Williams, in *Text and Dialogues: On Philosophy, Politics and Culture,* edited and with an introduction by Hugh J. Silverman and James Barry Jr., translated by Michael B. Smith et al., 74–84. Atlantic Highlands, N.J.: Humanities Press, 1992]. Lagrasse: Verdier, 1996.
RC	*Résumés de cours: Collège de France, 1952–1960.* Paris: Gallimard, 1968. ["Themes from the Lectures at the Collège de France, 1952–1960," in *In Praise of Philosophy and Other Essays,* translated by John Wild and James Edie, 71–198. Evanston, Ill.: Northwestern University Press, 1988.]
S	"Structure." In *Sens et usages du terme structure dans les sciences humaines et sociales,* edited by Roger Bastide. The Hague: Mouton, 1962. Summary of a lecture delivered at a colloquium on January 11, 1961. Repr. in *P2,* 317–20.
SC	*La structure du comportement.* Paris: Presses Universitaires de France, 1942. [*The Structure of Behavior.* Translated by

Alden L. Fisher. Foreword by John Wild. Boston: Beacon Press, 1963.]

SG   *Signes*. Paris: Gallimard, 1960. [*Signs*. Translated with an introduction by Richard S. McCleary. Evanston, Ill.: Northwestern University Press, 1964.]

SNS   *Sens et non-sens*. 1948. Paris: Gallimard, 1996. [*Sense and Non-Sense*. Translated with a preface by Hubert Dreyfus and Patricia Allen Dreyfus. Evanston, Ill.: Northwestern University Press, 1964.]

VI   *Le visible et l'invisible*. Followed by working notes. Edited with a foreword and afterword by Claude Lefort. Paris: Gallimard, 1964. [*The Visible and the Invisible, followed by Working Notes*. Edited by Claude Lefort. Translated by Alphonso Lingis. Evanston, Ill.: Northwestern University Press, 1968.]

The light dove, whilst in its free flight it divides the air, whose resistance it feels, might embrace the idea that it would succeed much better in airless space. Just in the same way, Plato abandoned the sensible world because it set such narrow limits to the understanding, and hazarded himself beyond it, upon the wings of his ideas, into the void space of the pure understanding. He did not remark, that he made no way by his efforts, since he had no resistance, as it were for support, whereupon he could rest, and whereby he could apply his powers, in order to make understanding move onward.
—**Immanuel Kant,** *Critique of Pure Reason,* **trans. Francis Haywood**

I strike matches—which do not light.
That is a *resistance.*
Impatience overtakes me.
This becomes a poem. Lack of success becomes a very sensible thing.
—**Paul Valéry,** *Cahiers*

Introduction: Return to the Obvious

The Science of the Obvious

Throughout his oeuvre, Maurice Merleau-Ponty returned incessantly to a single fundamental question: What does it mean to perceive? As he eventually observed in his radio lecture series, published under the title *The World of Perception* (1948), the perceptual world remains "to a great extent, unknown territory" (*C*, 11/39).[1] It has remained largely uncharted for two major reasons. The first is historical: Philosophy, because of its traditional distrust of the senses, has often neglected to undertake a sufficiently detailed investigation into the ways in which we perceive. The preference given to rational, abstract, and transindividual theory, to the detriment of situated, practical, and embodied knowledge, explains why perception has often remained beyond the purview of most philosophical investigations. The second reason, even more worrisome than the internal biases of the traditional Western order of knowledge, is that the meaning of perception remains opaque not only to the rationalist but also, and arguably even more so, to those taking a practical approach.

The "world of perception" will remain unknown territory, says Merleau-Ponty, "as long as we remain in a practical or utilitarian attitude" (*C*, 11/39). This attitude, naturalistic so to speak, may lead us to forget the perceptual situation. Practical engagement in the perceptual world may be the least apparent way of remaining unaware of it, but it may also be the most authoritative. Granted, few would doubt that most of our actions, assessments, and judgments involve a perceptual dimension in one way or another. Most would agree that to perform a task, realize a goal, or solve a practical problem, our bodily, sensorial capacities come into play at some level. It simply sounds trivial to say so: Such an awareness is rarely of any use in accomplishing the task at hand. And it is even more trivial to philosophical thought.

What does it mean to ask this seemingly trivial question? Why choose perception—of an apple, a tree, a bird—as a starting point for all further inquiries? In the first place, such a decision marks this starting point as something that does not go without saying. All philosophies (including the most systematic or deductive) must struggle with the innate flaw of having to begin somewhere; only in retrospect can an attempt be made to justify the contingent decision of one starting point over another. Maurice Merleau-Ponty begins with the perceptual situation, and throughout his inquiries he returns to it repeatedly. But though this starting point is no less contingent than any other (after all, why not start with God, the absolute, or the mathematical idea?), it differs from other philosophical beginnings in that the situation in which something is being perceived is overtly trivial, so trivial that it might seem to undermine the very pertinence of any philosophical starting point at all. Furthermore, this new beginning does not claim to lie deeper or to clear the ground for a new Archimedean point on which a solid conceptual edifice could then be erected. There is nothing less solid than the situation of perception. Accordingly, it is paradoxical to begin there: To a certain extent, it must be acknowledged that the ground on which all subsequent analyses will be built will never be foundational, since something so inherently trivial hardly qualifies as such.

When we ask what it means to perceive an apple on a table, in what sense is the question philosophical rather than physiological, optical, or psychological? We have "perceptual evidence" (*évidence perceptive*), Merleau-Ponty says, of the apple we see. By "evidence," he does not mean legal proof or some ultimate instrument of certainty. Rather, we take it for granted that what we see is an apple, and, should we be sitting around the same table, we usually have no reason to communicate the information that there is an apple on the table. We simply assume that we share the same perceptual space of reference. In our everyday experiences, we generally have no reason to state the obvious.

Still, it is precisely what appears most obvious, what is most apparent, that will serve as the starting point—contingent, to be sure—for Merleau-Ponty's phenomenology of perception. Perception should not be conceived as a more fundamental level or as merely a regional problem within a broader project called "phenomenology" (similar to the "philosophy of mathematics" or the "philosophy of religion," for example). To begin with perception, the most obvious and trivial situation, is at the same time to pursue Edmund Husserl's own understanding of phenomenology.

Edmund Husserl, the German philosopher and founder of phenomenology, once said, only half-jokingly, that philosophy should ultimately allow itself to become the "science of the trivial" (*Wissenschaft von den Trivialitäten*). He was thereby calling on philosophy to return to the banal, ordinary experience of things. The philosopher "must surely know that it is precisely behind the obvious that the hardest problems lie hidden, that this is so much so, in fact, that philosophy may be paradoxically, but not unprofoundly, called the science of the trivial. In the present case at least what seems at first quite trivial, reveals itself, on closer examination, as the source of deep-lying, widely ramifying problems."[2] Husserl is describing the pitfalls implicit in the endeavor to clarify the obvious. What is all too self-evident deserves no special mention; what is ordinary is too routine to stand out.

Husserl calls this the "obviousness" (*Selbstverständlichkeit*) of the everyday. The radical problem, he explains in the *Prague Lectures*, "is precisely the obviousness [*Selbstverständlichkeit*] in which the world is and is this world."[3] In this sense, the problem with obviousness is that it is considered unproblematic. There is a direct link between Husserl's concern and that of Merleau-Ponty, who repeatedly voices the need to "learn to see the world anew" (*réapprendre à voir le monde*). That need begins with the seemingly trivial circumstance that seeing the world anew means acknowledging that the world is something we *see*. "The world is what I perceive": In this statement, as so often in Merleau-Ponty, we symptomatically shift back and forth between an uncontroversial truism and a philosophical claim. "The world is what I perceive, but as soon as we examine and express its absolute proximity, it also becomes, inexplicably, irremediable distance" (*VI*, 17/8). To say that the world is everything that is perceptible, that—as the realm of the sensible—it comprises everything that can be an object of sensation, is to turn the sensible into something detached analytically from the subject engaged in it. But that seems counterintuitive: "The perceived thing is paradoxical; it exists only in so far as someone can perceive it" (*PrP*, 50/16). Conversely, perception cannot be fully reintegrated into the orbit of the perceiver. Perception is hardly a private activity confined within the jurisdiction of an inner self, since any perception is an opening toward something beyond itself. What remains to be done, Merleau-Ponty concludes, is to acknowledge the paradoxical nature of the perceptual situation. "Perception is thus paradoxical. . . . I cannot even for an instant imagine an object in itself" (PrP, 50/16).

This passage exemplifies an experience with which many of Merleau-Ponty's readers are familiar: To read Merleau-Ponty is to shift constantly from accounts of easily recognizable experiences to bold theoretical statements. Within the very same sentence, we have moved from a succession of descriptions that appear self-evident to a bold philosophical thesis, though we are unable to say in retrospect where the change in level exactly occurred. Such experiences of reading make the ways in which Merleau-Ponty understood Husserl's definition of phenomenology to be a "science of the trivial" all the more conspicuous. The reader is constantly turning toward concrete experiential situations; at the same time, what had seemed familiar becomes something startling. It is as if Merleau-Ponty felt it necessary to show the counterintuitive nature of Husserl's own call for a reappraisal of what is commonly held to be obvious—what the Greeks called the *doxa*—which would make the return to the *doxa* ultimately indistinguishable from the transformation of the obvious into *paradoxa*.

Adversity: What Is in the Way

In the preface to *Phenomenology of Perception,* Merleau-Ponty argues that "we must—precisely in order to see the world and to grasp it as a paradox—rupture our familiarity with it" (PP, xiv/lxxvi). That is no easy task, however, given the elusive character of the ordinary. Strategies must be found to counter the anesthetizing power of routine and, in the face of unquestioned presuppositions, to tear off the blinding veil of familiarity. In a sense, this endeavor coincides with the philosophical project as a whole, and it should be remembered that Socrates' disruptive effect was compared by the Athenians to a torpedo fish's electric shock.[4] When Merleau-Ponty evokes the need to see the world as if we were seeing it for the first time, while loosening "the intentional threads that connect us to the world in order to make them appear" (PP, xiv/lxxvi), he repeats the gesture characteristic of virtually all critical philosophies: that of methodologically bracketing the ordinary. In another sense, however, Merleau-Ponty's questioning of the obvious differs from a traditional (e.g., Cartesian) skepticism.

When Merleau-Ponty says that our bodily engagement with the world always presupposes a "perceptual faith" (*foi perceptive*), his aim is not to pillory an unjustified or groundless belief but rather to understand its nature. The embodied, perceiving subject considers the apple that one sees on the table not as sense datum, not as a representation or simulacrum;

one believes there really is an apple on the table to which perception gives one access. To take the skeptic's stance and suspend the sensorial evidence in the search for some unshakable truth beyond appearances would once again be to dismiss the paradoxical nature of all phenomena and to split the world into *noumena* and *phainomena*, essences and appearances. The skeptic's attitude toward what appears stems from a deep-rooted fear of contingency, which ultimately leads to reintroducing dualism into experience.

In this regard Merleau-Ponty, in his rebuttal of skepticism, is very close to Husserl, who already emphasized that the return to phenomenal appearances had to be understood as a realist stance: "There can be no stronger realism than this, if by this word we mean 'I am certain of being a human being who lives in this world, etc., and I doubt it not in the least.' But the greatest problem is precisely to understand what is here so 'obvious.'"[5] In line with his outspoken rejection of metaphysical inquiries and his focus on why what appears to be obvious does in fact appear obvious, Husserl advised a method of investigation he called *reduction*, which, in its various modalities and implications, became the subject of many later discussions within phenomenology. Merleau-Ponty considers Husserl's principle of reduction a crucial contribution to philosophy, yet his praise takes a peculiar turn, thereby indicating the point at which Merleau-Ponty diverges from Husserl. "The most important lesson of the [phenomenological] reduction," Merleau-Ponty summarizes in the preface to *Phenomenology of Perception*, "is the impossibility of a complete reduction" (*PP*, 14/lxxvi).

This statement is especially puzzling in that it comes in the middle of what looks like praise of Husserl's method. To tease out what might be intended by such a statement, we may find it helpful to recall that, in phenomenology, "reduction" does not mean "simplification"; rather, it is quite literally the name for a method that intends to "lead back" (Latin *re-ducere, reductio*) to the origin. Within Husserlian phenomenology, a long-lasting debate has raged over whether Husserl wanted to retrace the transcendental condition of appearances to the transcendental self (the *Cogito*) or rather to the lifeworld of things (some even introduced a third, middle term, the "psychological way"). I discuss some of the aspects of this debate in chapter 1 in the section titled "The Problem of Transcendence." For now, suffice it to say that, already in *Phenomenology of Perception*, Merleau-Ponty anticipates his later position, condemning the fantasy of reverting to an ultimate, positive position, the transcendental *Cogito*, for example. "For a long time, and even in recent texts, the reduction has been presented as the return to a transcendental consciousness in front of which the world is spread out in an absolute transparency, animated throughout by a series of apperceptions whose reconstitution, beginning from their results, is the task of the philosopher" (*PP*, v/lxxiv–lxxv, trans. modified). But to lead everything back to the positivity of the empirical lifeworld is once again to fall short of what experience is. Ultimately, the figure of *chiasm,* introduced in the late 1950s, will allow Merleau-Ponty to move closer to this intrinsic nonpositivity of things, which he will come to call "reversibility."

Merleau-Ponty's phenomenology is also realist, and on this point he takes the side of Husserl's antiskepticism (already at an early stage, Merleau-Ponty makes an appeal to "define transcendental philosophy in such a way as to integrate it with the very phenomenon of the real" (*SC*, 241/224); yet his choice to begin the philosophical analysis with the situation of perception makes him wary of the dangers of an "intellectualized realism." Husserl calls for the willful suspension of judgment—the *epoché*, or "bracketing," of all assumptions—with regard to everything that appears to a consciousness, but Merleau-Ponty sees this move as still too firmly anchored in the neutral realm of the intellect. The obviousness of the obvious is not only called into question by a willful decision; it may also occur in an abrupt or undesired manner.

When Husserl claims that the obvious (*das Selbstverständliche*) is not sufficiently understood for itself (*verstanden als es selbst*), he is still operating solely within the realm of reason (*Verstand*). In response to the skeptic, Husserl had to demonstrate why the question "What is it that I know?" should not be posed in terms of metaphysics but with respect to a specific, situated experience. Merleau-Ponty changes the question to "What is it that I see?" and this object-oriented, concrete approach instantly seems more natural, since it is a question that perceivers ask on a daily basis. It could be claimed that, through his descriptions of situations, Merleau-Ponty wants to evoke familiar settings for experiences that suddenly change their aspect without any methodological intervention taking place. Like Husserl, he favors a return to the *doxa,* but he does so only to distinguish the moment when the "doxical" unexpectedly turns into the paradoxical: The return to the obvious amounts to a re-turn, a new twist, of the obvious. In Merleau-Ponty's texts, the everyday meaning of the question "What is it that I see?" becomes almost indistinguishable from a philosophical inquiry—and that might well be deliberate.

All this entails a reconfiguration of the very notion of the "obvious." Generally speaking, what is held to be obvious does not stand out. It is passed over, since there is no reason to pause on it: Customs, habits, and standardization have smoothed out its rough edges, and, as we know from experience, things that are patently familiar tend quickly to become normative (at best, we ask ourselves silently: "How could it be otherwise?").

The obvious is not what can be understood without further ado but rather what is not even the object of understanding, because it is not reflected on in the first place: What is obvious has become so quotidian that its very obviousness eludes us. It is worth remembering, however, that the Latin word *obvius*, the source of our modern "obvious," signifies the opposite of a smoothed-out ground: *Obvius* comes from *ob viam*, which is to say, what is in the way or over against (its meaning survives in the verb *obviate*, which means to prevent from leaping forward, to anticipate what will be in the way). In Latin one would say, when something comes to the fore or comes to meet us, that it is *obviam ire*, it comes into or gets in our way. In a literal sense, then, the obvious is not what goes unnoticed but what meets the eye and brings insight to a halt.

To begin with the perceptual situation—even to claim against all odds a "primacy of perception" (the title of one of Merleau-Ponty's earliest texts)—is to give more space within philosophy to what is permanently in the way. Whereas, for Aristotle, the greatest promise of the contemplative life lies at the far end of a continuum of thinking (*noēsis noēseōs*, the "thinking of thinking" without the intrusion of anything else), perception is only possible when something eludes our grasp. To become perceptible, a thing must always already appear against a field that recedes into the background (if everything were visible at once, no "thing" in particular could be seen); the object appears only because one of its aspects comes to the fore, overshadowing all the others, which become imperceptible by the very act of perception. The perceiving subject may move around a spherical object (an apple, for example) as often as he or she pleases but will never have it completely surrounded; unlike an abstract geometrical sphere, which is complete in itself, the sensible always already resists being thoroughly enclosed.

In the following chapters, I would like to introduce Merleau-Ponty's thinking by means of this motif of the intrinsic *resistance of the sensible*. Merleau-Ponty describes it first with reference to the experience of perception, and later, within the context of his "ontological turn," he generalizes it to the experiential world as a whole. To say that the sensible has a resistance of its own is to claim that it is more than a neutral substratum of sense data. Yet that is also very different from defining it as a *res extensa*: The sensible is not reducible to a set of properties (e.g., "inertia," as defined by physics), nor is it merely a support for (or correlate of) an intention. Merleau-Ponty sometimes calls this resistance an "adversity" (*adversité*)— from *ad versus*, "turned toward, turned around"—which is, once again, what stands in the way. But instead of understanding what stands in the way as a historical counterforce (dialectical history in the Marxist sense) or as a clearly defined antagonistic entity (Descartes's malignant demon), we should conceive of Merleau-Ponty's adversity as the prevailing condition of sensible experience as such. "When our initiatives get stuck in the glue of the body, of language, or of that world beyond measure which is given to us to finish, it is not that a *malin génie* sets his will against us; it is only a matter of a sort of inertia, a passive resistance, a dying fall of meaning—an anonymous adversity" (*SG*, 304/239, trans. modified). Merleau-Ponty's understanding of the "return to things themselves" thus literally signifies the becoming-sensible of thought, a coming to grips with the solid facticity of what is. In that respect, he inflects a certain tendency present in Husserlian phenomenology, which is to conceive of an orientation toward experience as a kind of *transcendence* or "moving beyond." The notion of adversity first appears in Merleau-Ponty's manuscripts in 1947 in reaction to the antiphenomenological argument put forward by Gaston Bachelard in *Earth and Reveries of Will* the same year. Bachelard criticizes phenomenology— including Merleau-Ponty's *Phenomenology of Perception* (1945)—for being obsessed with "oriented intentionality" and for not sufficiently taking into account what he calls the "coefficient of adversity" (*coefficient d'adversité*). In place of a "philosophy of the toward" (*philosophie du vers*), says Bachelard, what is called for above all else is a "philosophy of the against" (*philosophie du contre*).[6]

Merleau-Ponty, who had read Bachelard extensively, seems to have taken this admonition very seriously, though he was also aware of the difficulties of thinking along the lines of or in the grip of what resists. To turn resistance into a positive concept or quality would inevitably be to efface its resistant character and make it something that perfectly fit the mold of the concept. A concept of resistance that would mount no opposition to being conceptualized would be only faintly resistant; conversely, a philosophy that turns all sensible things into entities that repel contact entirely would negate the reality of sensible experience. How, then, to give an account of the experience of *contact*, that is, both a familiarity with the fabric of things and their perpetual withdrawal, a moving toward that always already implies that the object we seek to attain is receding into the depths of the perceptual field. The word "phenomenology" assumes its most literal sense here: It signifies the struggle to "give an account" (*logon didonai*) of how phenomena occur to us.

As Merleau-Ponty explained in the mid-1950s, it is this problem "that every theory of perception runs up against; consequently the explication of perceptual experience must make us acquainted with a genus of being with regard to which the subject is not sovereign" (*IP*, 267/206). In comments at a colloquium titled "Husserl's Works and Thought" in April 1957, he again revised the notion of adversity, henceforth defining it as the very "resistance of the unreflected to reflection" (*HCR*, 159). Unlike Martin Heidegger, whose work he would increasingly grapple with in those years, Merleau-Ponty did not seek to uncover a more fundamental, insufficiently reflected level of Being; rather, he sought to acknowledge that all sensible experience is inherently perspectival. If a thing resists reflection, that is not because it has remained insufficiently thought, but because there is a blind spot in any engagement—perceptual or intellectual—with the world. By virtue of the constitutive incompleteness of all perception, the act of seeing always entails seeing anew. And if one concedes that conceptual sense (signification) also occurs within the sensible and that there is a connection between sensibility and intelligence (after all, don't we say things like "it would be more sensible to act like this or that"?), the same will be true for thinking: Just as there is a *punctum caecum* on the retina, which is both a gap in vision and its precondition, any investigation of the sensible world will also have its blind spot. Every new unveiling of an aspect can at best move around that blind spot: It can never abolish it. In this respect, resistance is not a quality belonging to an object (like density or compactness, for example) but the experience of something that escapes our grasp of it and cannot be objectified. Resistance is the symptom of a negativity inherent in the experiential field; it is what opens up a distance within proximity and creates depth. To quote Merleau-Ponty, it is "because of depth that things have flesh: that is, they set up obstacles to my inspection, a resistance which is precisely their reality, their 'openness,' their *totum simul*" (*VI*, 239/216, trans. modified).

How to Read Merleau-Ponty?

In a passage written near the end of his life, Merleau-Ponty recalls that, for Plato, philosophy begins with *thaumazein*, amazement:[7] "Philosophy is *thaumazein*, that is, the consciousness of bewilderment [*la conscience de l'étrangeté*]" (*P2*, 365). Bewilderment or estrangement, however, occurs only in relation to a given, familiar context; what is absolutely different is so disconnected (*ab-solutus*) from experience that it can produce only indifference. As a result, Merleau-Ponty says, the return to the seemingly obvious necessarily entails a radicalization of the perplexing power of what was thought to be near and the experience of distance as a concrete withdrawal of experience, something that rarely happens in the well-oiled machinery of philosophical discourse. In reality, "philosophy only breathes when it rejects infinitely infinite thinking in order to see the world in its strangeness" (*P2*, 370).

I argue that the claim Merleau-Ponty makes about the world should also be applied to him. Many think—erroneously—that his philosophy is an easy read, that it lacks many of the constraints of other, more technical philosophical systems. In a nutshell, *reading Merleau-Ponty has become too obvious*. For a mode of thought that was suddenly cut short by Merleau-Ponty's premature death in 1961, it has displayed surprising durability, attracting increasingly more attention as the decades pass. Merleau-Ponty has become an almost inevitable reference point, one of the major figures not only of phenomenology but of philosophy as a whole. Two general attitudes have prevailed: the *mimetic* and the *decontextualizing*. The mimetic attitude is typical of interpreters (especially in the French-speaking world) who, in response to Merleau-Ponty's seductive writing, have been tempted to imitate his train of thought and to emulate his style. It is indeed easy to be caught up in enthusiasm for his refreshingly luminous and lithe prose. The risk, however, is that in mimicking his writing style to perfection, his imitators will flatten all that made for its contrasts and asperities.

The other attitude (particularly prevalent in the English-speaking world but existing in many other places as well) is equally perilous: the decontextualizing attitude takes Merleau-Ponty's oeuvre as a kind of open-air quarry from which arguments or concepts can be randomly extracted, regardless of the context in which they appear. Some of Merleau-Ponty's notions have by now attained the status of fetish concepts; like brilliant gems, they have been carved and polished in such a way as to make their provenance completely unrecognizable. Merleau-Ponty's oeuvre, caught between those who link a philosopher's potency to the number of epigones who mimic his style and those who believe that its relevance can be measured only by isolating the argument from its original context, between a devout attitude that supposedly extends the author's intentions beyond his own text and an attitude of high-handed self-interest, has seldom been the object of a thorough, systematic interpretation. Hampered by readings from too remote or too close a vantage point, it stands in need of studies that will bring out the immanent coherence that the oeuvre retains throughout all its evolutions.

In light of this dual risk, my question will be the following: How are we to read Merleau-Ponty? How to identify the lines of force without effacing those rough spots, which, in fact, are merely their visible expression? To read Merleau-Ponty anew is necessarily to restore a kind of resistance to his text. All too often that resistance, coming in the wake of so many previous readings, has been smoothed out: His thought has become too recognizable, too obvious. To release the potential of his oeuvre to prompt new thoughts, I propose to circumscribe these zones of contact where reflection can occur, approaching and retreating from the fractiousness and friction that can spark ideas. And to read Merleau-Ponty, we must also read what he himself was reading. Not surprisingly, he sought contact with philosophical authors very different from himself (Descartes and Leibniz, for instance), sought the resistance of other natural or social sciences: phonology, zoology, developmental psychology, psychiatry. Although he classified his later thinking as an *intra-* or *endo*-ontology, this ought not to be taken as a return to "interiority" or to an immanence of the first-person point of view. There is no such thing as an "inner man," Merleau-Ponty states unmistakably (*PP*, xi/lxxiv), and "consciousness has no private life" (*PP*, 52/30). For Merleau-Ponty, the starting point of the experience of a situated, embodied, perceiving subject cannot be cut off from other perspectives; rather, it is the only way to acknowledge that experience is always already pervaded by something that inherently escapes appropriation (the experience we call our own is nothing we could in good faith claim to be our own; or to put it somewhat bluntly, experiences are not something we make the way we might make a cake). If it turns out that most of what we count as our experience is not something for which we can claim authorship (let alone ownership), all the other instances that shape experience and its meaning have to be taken into account. In this respect, as Merleau-Ponty surmises, "What we know of ourselves is much more indebted to the external knowledge of the historical past, of ethnography, of mental pathology, for instance, than to the direct elucidation of our own life" (*P2*, 12).

Merleau-Ponty's progress—which I retrace in this book—from the study of socially embodied behavior to the "intra-ontology" of the flesh by no means coincides with an exclusion of the "Outside." Rather, Merleau-Ponty takes his inspiration from experimental science, political institutions, historical events, artistic practices, and literary works.[8] A comprehensive analysis of these specific encounters makes it clear that the best response to the skeptic's doubts about the existence of the world is not to formulate an intellectual argument—which the skeptic could easily dispute—but rather to situate thinking within the entanglements of the real. As Merleau-Ponty says, when we start with the experience of something that resists full apprehension, we move beyond the false alternative between the third- and the first-person points of view: "not outside of us and not in us, but there where the two movements cross, where 'there is' something" (*VI*, 210/95, trans. modified).

To recapture the singularity of Merleau-Ponty's thinking, I situate his philosophical operations within their philosophical and nonphilosophical contexts, pointing out both the continuities and the discontinuities. First and foremost, I have assumed that Merleau-Ponty's oeuvre, however aporetic and open-ended, displays an internal coherence, which lies not necessarily in its subjects of inquiry but in its method. Every oeuvre—and a philosophical oeuvre is no exception—proceeds by zigzags, leaps and retreats, breakthroughs and returns. The interpreter's task is therefore to remain faithful to the organic development and natural dynamics of that oeuvre. At the same time, however, the interpreter must point out the gaps that, having been diligently effaced by retrospective self-interpretations, remain invisible in any linear reconstruction.

In view of this double imperative, the three chapters that constitute the body of this book should be read both synchronically and diachronically. In chapter 1, I locate the origin of Merleau-Ponty's insistence on the *perceptual nature of being* in his early debates with psychology and behavioral science, arguing for the gradual emergence in his oeuvre of a specifically phenomenological account of perceptual experience. In chapter 2, I focus on the progressive broadening of Merleau-Ponty's scope from the situation of the embodied, kinesthetic self to the problem of *expression*: Although there can be no expression without embodiment of a certain kind, the general phenomenon of expression cannot be derived from a description of the kinesthetic "I." Expression, as a transindividual phenomenon, requires a level of ideality, which led Merleau-Ponty—by means of a detour through structural linguistics—to desubjectivize his philosophy somewhat. One of the claims I make in this book is that the middle phase, with the specific importance it grants to the linguistic phenomenon, is crucial for understanding the later ontological turn. The reasons for Merleau-Ponty's peculiar decision to introduce an ontological understanding of sensible experience are laid out in chapter 3, and the correlative notions of "flesh" and "chiasm" are explained in detail. In that chapter I also discuss the key importance of visual experience, with the "proximity in distance" it entails, for the genesis of Merleau-Ponty's ontology of sensible difference.

There is one trope that keeps surfacing in his oeuvre, something like the "thread between the simultaneous and the successive" (*VI*, 172/114, trans. modified): This is his *critique of any ideology of transparency*, whether it be the self's transparency to itself, the transparency of knowledge to the self, or the transparency to the self of others. Strangely enough, this notion of transparency has until now been largely overlooked, even though (unlike some other notions, such as "flesh" and "chiasm") it is already present in the earliest writings and persists to the end. That notion, without ever acquiring the status of a concept—remaining, therefore, below the rank of philosophical ennoblement—does not appear in any glossary of Merleau-Pontian terms. And yet we need only pay some attention to the texts to realize how frequently it recurs. Usually appearing in its adjectival form, the notion of the "transparent" generally serves a critical purpose, crystallizing what philosophy has so often overlooked: *The fiction of transparency expresses in a nutshell the forgetting or oblivion of the material a priori, that is, the constitutive corporeal mediateness of any relationship to the world.*

My aim in this book is therefore twofold: to introduce Merleau-Ponty's oeuvre to those unacquainted with it and to allow those already versed in it new access to its deeper implications. In particular, I compare some well-known passages to working notes that have yet to be published. The organization of the book into three chapters roughly corresponds to what most commentators consider the internal articulation of Merleau-Ponty's oeuvre, into an "early," "middle," and "late" phase. Although the initial framework of the perceptual situation is never abandoned, it undergoes two major modifications, the "expressivist turn" and the "ontological turn." The reasons for these shifts are retraced in the following chapters, in order to set out the corresponding continuities and discontinuities in Merleau-Ponty's thought. At the same time, each chapter is organized around a specific concept that, within each phase, stands for a particular critique of transparency and opens the dimension of the constitutive mediateness of appearance. In chapter 1, this concept is *milieu*, borrowed from the behavioral sciences and endowed with a new meaning. In chapter 2, the "expressivist turn" and the encounter with linguistics, Ferdinand de Saussure's in particular, give rise to the concept of the *diacritical,* whose importance has never been fully recognized. In chapter 3, I investigate the reasons for the "ontological turn," developing a concept of *flesh* that should be understood not as a positive, physical entity but as the ontological fabric of the visible world. At the same time, I indicate the important role that Merleau-Ponty's engagement with painting, that of Cézanne in particular, played in this speculative process.

In the conclusion, departing from the fidelity of a historical reconstruction, I inquire into the philosophical legacy of an oeuvre left unfinished, broken off abruptly, available to us now only in fragmented form. Despite conceptual and speculative turning points with wide-ranging consequences, Merleau-Ponty never did give up the initial context of the perceptual situation; he continued to delve ever deeper into its implications. It is worth asking what it would mean to continue where Merleau-Ponty left off. The final working notes open several avenues of thought, anticipating later developments in twentieth- and twenty-first-century philosophy but also yielding possibilities for a new kind of philosophy. One idea, certainly, must be renounced: that phenomenology provides immediate access to things. If anything, Merleau-Ponty's rejection of transparency introduces a subtle but decisive shift: Although all that appears perceptually appears *in it-self*, this does not mean it appears *immediately*. All appearance—this would be Merleau-Ponty's point—appears *through* something else, by virtue of which it receives its meaning; all appearance is a *trans-appearance*. Against this backdrop, a different perspective emerges on the so-called ontological turn in the later work, which has caused major difficulties for many interpreters: Much of the problem disappears when the ominous "flesh of the world" is no longer thought of as an extension of the body but as a medium in its own right. Merleau-Ponty's last, unfinished writings thus gesture toward a conception that comes very close to an idea developed in Aristotle: that of the *diaphanous* nature of the sensible. The investigation of phenomena—phenomenology—must become a dia-phenomenology.

1

Perception

(Dis)avowal of Science

"Back to the things themselves!" (*Zurück zu den Sachen selbst*): Such is Edmund Husserl's famous battle cry for the phenomenological movement. That return to things means climbing down from the unassailable position of pure thought, which Ludwig Wittgenstein, the other great figure of the twentieth century's philosophical revival, called "slippery ice," where "conditions are ideal, but . . . we are unable to walk."[1] Husserl's injunction, powerful in its impetus but vague in its direction, becomes more concrete when it is explained, to borrow Wittgenstein's words once again, as a "return to the rough ground" (*Zurück auf den rauhen Boden!*).[2] From the start, the rough ground Merleau-Ponty sought was that of the perceptual situation. Although the question is at work across the entire arc of his philosophy, it is possible to distinguish a first phase—extending from approximately 1933 until 1945—when the problem of the nature of perception constituted the guiding thread of his thinking. Merleau-Ponty, taking an interest almost from the first in the new results of experimental psychology, became particularly aware of the question of the perceptual through writings in Gestalt psychology, which he studied systematically. In 1933 or 1934, he began work on a thesis that would concern the nature of behavior. His requests for grants from the Caisse Nationale des Sciences reveal the driving force behind a line of research that would persist until *Phenomenology of Perception*.[3] The originality that can already be glimpsed in these grant proposals is manifest in a bibliography filled with works on psychology, neurology, and psychiatry, at the expense of philosophy (no classic author appears on it). But though Merleau-Ponty thumbs his nose at academia, which was dominated at the time by idealism and French neo-Kantianism, he does not bid philosophy adieu, since he will be quick to declare his disagreement not with the object of science but with its methods. The thesis proposal asserts the irreducibility of the perceptual world to scientific epistemology: "The universe of perception could not be assimilated to the universe of science" (*PrP*, 13/75). *Phenomenology of Perception* is even more explicit, beginning with an apodictic and puzzling statement: "Phenomenology . . . is first and foremost the disavowal of science" (*PP*, ii/lxxi).

What are we to make of this assertion? Does not Merleau-Ponty fall into the trap of the same intellectualist philosophies he denounces in these lines? But we must first agree on what that "disavowal" means. Merleau-Ponty explains himself on that count with reference to Husserl's own approach: It is not that phenomenology should be "indifferent" to the empirical sciences and psychology (*PrP*, 21/77) but that it must avoid modeling itself on their method. "It is a matter of renewing psychology *on its own terrain*, of bringing to life *the methods proper to it* by analyses which fix the persistently uncertain meaning of fundamental essences, such as 'representation,' 'memory,' etc." (*PrP*, 22–23/78). When Husserl—and Merleau-Ponty as well—criticizes psychology, he hardly does so to call into question the legitimacy of an inductive approach; rather, he seeks to shore it up with an eidetic approach. There is unquestionably a continuity between *The Structure of Behavior*, the first book that emerged from Merleau-Ponty's reflections in contact with the sciences, and *Phenomenology of Perception* (1945). In the earlier work, published in 1942 but already completed in 1938, he attempts to conceive of perception with and against science; in the second, he radicalizes that movement while making an effort to identify what science assumes and what, qua assumption, remains its unthought—the lived experience of the sensible world. In the preface, he maintains that "if we wish to think science rigorously, to appreciate precisely its sense and its scope, we must first awaken that experience of the world of which science is the second-order expression" (*PP*, iii/lxxii).

Before we arrive at the question of primordial expression—the subject of my next chapter—let me insist once again on the unitary aim of that entire first phase but also on the differences at work. Whereas *The Structure of Behavior* takes a negative path, insisting on why a phenomenological approach cannot be reduced to behavioral psychology, *Phenomenology of Perception* seeks to elaborate a positive account of the life of the embodied subject. The first book seeks, according to the explanation that Merleau-Ponty himself gives, to determine the sense (or nonsense) of an approach that considers the human being "from the point of view of the disinterested onlooker" (*P2*, 12), whereas the second, "placing itself within the subject" (*P2*, 13), brings to light the unthought, that is, experience, on the basis of experience itself. When we consider these two works side by side, we discover a chiasm: Where *Phenomenology of Perception* belongs fundamentally to a mode of thinking from inside experience and places positive knowledge in a position of exteriority, *The Structure of Behavior* does not yet situate itself within an experiential perspective but rather argues from within scientific discourse, producing a critique of the sciences that is paradoxically informed by these same disciplines.[4]

That interpretation may grant too much weight to Merleau-Ponty's later efforts in 1951 to reconcile the arguments in his previous books in support of his pending candidacy for a position at the Collège de France (one cannot fail to observe the conceptual evolution that occurred between *The Structure of Behavior* and *Phenomenology of Perception*). In its intentions, however, the earlier book already brings about a radical displacement of the philosophical milieu within which Merleau-Ponty sought to speak. As a result, it reactivates the problem of the relation between body and soul—since, of course, it is this old problem that is, once again, at stake. And it does so without trudging through the aporias of the tradition. Rather, it installs itself from the start within scientific debate, which carefully avoids these metaphysical dichotomies. It raises once again the question of the relation between activity and passivity, not reducing them to the subject-object duality but analyzing what precedes that distinction, namely, *behavior*. In that sense, behavior is less the book's theme—which is already and still perception—than its strategic apparatus. In opting for the scientific domain, then, Merleau-Ponty already distinguishes his thought from an intellectualist philosophy that dissolves perception into "thinking about perception." In taking behavior as a shortcut across the field of the empirical sciences, he already chooses a path that will allow him to arrive at his object, experience proper.[5] For the moment, however, let us remain within the layout of *The Structure of Behavior*. In it Merleau-Ponty studies very heterogeneous concepts one by one, still struggling to identify his own point of view, which has led a number of commentators to set aside that first book in favor of the second. I believe, however, that by 1933–38, when he was working on *The Structure of Behavior*, the critical perspective that would persist throughout all the different inquiries to which Merleau-Ponty subsequently dedicated himself was already taking shape: namely, a philosophy that *denounces any philosophy of transparency*. Although the term "transparency" does not yet have the value of an operative concept that it will later assume,[6] the motif is already undeniably present. In addition, the opacification of perception and its reinsertion into the life of the embodied subject, which will lead to *Phenomenology of Perception,* is no doubt the unifying moment of the disparate analyses of the earlier book.

Between the Mechanical and Gestalt

Like Husserl, who recommended beginning from a naïve attitude and from the "representations" we form of things, Merleau-Ponty, in this treatise on behavior from the vantage point of science, feels obliged to identify the doxa in the "scientific representation" of behavior (*SC*, 199/184). He starts by identifying the naïve attitude of classic science, which later returns under the designation "philosophy of causality." Although never developed in detail, that expression is used to stigmatize any position that trusts in the possibility of a direct, immediate, and linear action on an object. Such a philosophy understands the cause as a "constant and unconditioned antecedent" event (*SC*, 7/9), the necessary and sufficient condition for the effect to occur and thus always verifiable, provided it is isolated correctly. As a result, what presents itself as a coherent realism amounts merely to an atomism that dissects processes into so many independent links; the task is to eliminate the external elements to reach a pure relation whereby the cause unconditionally gives rise to the effect. And that causalism is in no way restricted to the physical world. Animal reflexology, to which Merleau-Ponty devotes a substantial part of the book, purports to include the physiological, but without doing away with the causalist postulate, which it in fact continues to embrace. In studying the instincts of dogs, Ivan Pavlov, the Russian physiologist, even broadens its domain, since he posits a direct action of the physical on the physiological. Pavlov's theory of reflexes would generate absurd extensions: From the moment this theory presupposes an original state of direct correspondence between stimulus and response, it is constrained to invent "inhibiting powers" that "interfere with" the transparency of the immediate reflex. The problem is insurmountable so long as behavior is conceived as the correlate of a reflex produced in an empty channel. Even when an interaction between different channels is posited, the existence of a constituted world with preestablished connections (*SC*, 35/35) is never questioned. Through that decomposition of the world into all its fixed connections, causalism becomes engulfed in interminable Zeno's paradoxes.

In *The Structure of Behavior,* Merleau-Ponty also discusses the philosophical positions that reject such a materialist atomism. He shows that, ultimately, they too still operate within the very system they reject. On the one hand, vitalism claims to reintroduce vital force where there is only mechanical force. Although that vital force evades the classic physicalist explanation, its effects must be reintegrated into the mechanical and turn out to be only a supplementary factor (SC, 149/138). As a result, vitalism paradoxically takes the forms of a "physics in the living being," without really managing to conceptualize the "physics of the living being" (SC, 164/151). On the other hand, intellectualism moves beyond the juxtapositions of atomism, but only to displace the sensible to the sphere of understanding. Given the heterogeneity of essence between the sensible and the perceived, there would no longer be a relation of contiguity but rather a relation of conformity. Neo-Kantian thought—strongly rooted in interwar France and Merleau-Ponty's target whenever he uses the term *criticisme*—would simply reduce perception to one mode of judgment among others (SC, 217/201). That prevents it from putting "consciousness in contact with an opaque and foreign reality" (SC, 283/224). In contrast to mechanistic philosophy, which understands behavior in terms of an initial state of transparency—and whose approach is not truly called into question by vitalism but rather confirmed by it—and in contrast to intellectualism, which reduces behavior to the instrument of an ideality, the key issue for Merleau-Ponty is to conceptualize the organization of the sensible in terms of perception. Contrary to any reductive doctrine, which, in the case of intellectualism, gives rise to a transparent model of thought and, in the case of mechanism, to a "mosaic" of sensations (here Merleau-Ponty is using Max Wertheimer's expression), he believes one must consider "the total 'image' of the organism" (SC, 22/23). He finds the principle for that comprehensive approach in Gestalt psychology, to which he will ceaselessly return until the last of his writings. Whereas materialist atomism claims to provide explanations on the basis of a fragmentation of the causal chains, the Gestalt school's credo is that the whole is always greater than the sum of its parts (SC, 49/47). Even if there truly is a distinction of the parts within the whole, these parts cannot be separated out, because they constitute an organic totality. Form (*Gestalt*) is neither in things nor in consciousness: It organizes their relation. Above all, it is structure.

Much later, at a conference on the word "structure" held in Paris in January 1959, Merleau-Ponty will provide a definition of that term that applies equally well to "form": Structure is an "internal principle of an observable distribution" (S, 154).[7] The emphasis is on "observable," since, contrary to the more common usage of the term by what is usually classified as "structuralism," this is not a structure underlying the world of the senses but a structure *within* the world of the senses. As such, it is constitutively *sensible*.

Even though, by virtue of the terms "form" and "structure" (often used interchangeably in *The Structure of Behavior*), a number of inherited forms of reductionism are swept aside, other difficulties persist. For Merleau-Ponty, the school of Kurt Koffka and Wolfgang Köhler tends to substantialize form, to abstract it from the real interactions of experience. Although he saw the research of the Gestalt theorists as "relieving neurologists of the task of looking for decals of mental functions on localized anatomical functions" (*PrP*, 12/74), any theory of form detached from the permanent readjustment processes involved in perception runs the risk of establishing in turn a new apriorism. The proof, if any were needed, consists of the few recurrent and canonical examples of visual forms appearing in the works of Gestalt theory, which risk placing form before its perception and of bringing an insidious comeback of Platonism. The Gestaltist approach, moreover, even if it rejects all idealism and resolutely locates forms in the immanence of the physical world, does not see that preestablished forms do not exist *in* the world; rather, forms are always already the *emergence* of a world. The formulation of *Phenomenology of Perception* is explicit: *Gestalt* "is the very appearance of the world, not its condition of possibility. It is the birth of a norm, not realized according to a norm" (*PP*, 74/62).

In chapter 4 of *The Structure of Behavior*, Merleau-Ponty thus shows that there can be no alphabet of symbolic forms, no order to preestablished elements, but only structured structures, which are at the same time always already structuring structures. Hence perceptual consciousness is neither the receptacle of that "life of forms" nor a duplicate of the structures of the world but rather the site of its emergence (*SC*, 157/145). In that sense, there is neither exteriority nor indifference between the sensible world and consciousness. The relation between consciousness and one's own body—Merleau-Ponty reminds us from the outset that this is what is at stake in *The Structure of Behavior*—is not an instrumental relation of "means" but an embeddedness in a "milieu." Consciousness is a "milieu of the universe," and phenomenology, as a science of what is given to consciousness, is an "inventory" of that milieu (*SC*, 215/199). Many have insisted—and rightly so—on the fecundity of these ideas, which would give rise in particular to the theory of the body as milieu and then to the theory of creative expressiveness. However, only a few have looked into the genesis of the vocabulary used here.

Milieu

In his use of the term "milieu," Merleau-Ponty was primarily inspired by the ethologist Jakob von Uexküll[8] and the psychopathologist Kurt Goldstein.[9] The word belongs to a long-standing tradition on which it would be worthwhile to pause. Paradoxically, the notion of milieu, used by Merleau-Ponty in his critique of mechanistic determinism, is itself derived from mechanics. It is essentially in that sense that it appears in Diderot and d'Alembert's *Encyclopédie*: "*Milieu*, noun, masculine (*Mech.*): in mechanical philosophy, it signifies a material space through which a body in motion passes, or in general, a material space in which a body is situated, whether or not it is moving." More exactly, the French term *milieu* is a translation of the English "medium," which Newton used to explain the phenomenon of action at a distance. Unlike Cartesian mechanics, which—as Merleau-Ponty will show in *Eye and Mind*—understands action in terms of "impact" (vision, the sensation at a distance par excellence, is explained through the analogy of the blind man's cane feeling out the surface of the ground and of objects), Newton believes that every action is produced in "fluid mediums." That so-called fluid medium, however, is still strictly determined by its physical properties. Therefore, the "resistance of the medium" in question in the entry of the *Encyclopédie* is associated with the physical "density" of the parts composing the medium. Air, water, and glass are given as examples.

That entry from the late eighteenth century, however, already contains the germ of what will become, in the nineteenth century, the behaviorist theory of the milieu. "Water," writes the author of the entry, "is a *milieu* in which fish live & move." It is this aspect that will attract the attention of Jean-Baptiste de Lamarck, the French biologist, who was deeply interested in *milieux* (the expression is always in the plural) such as water, air, and light. He draws from them his conception of "influencing circumstances," the set of factors that determine the organism from the outside. Léon Brunschvicg (whose courses Merleau-Ponty attended while studying at the École Normale Supérieure between 1926 and 1930) had revealed that the explanation for the living thing proposed by Lamarck is nothing other than a transformation into biological terms of the physico-mathematical system of Newton's "external interactions."[10] In that theory of the living milieu, the organism is thus exposed to action at a distance, in the sense that, through the intervention of *need,* the medium or milieu conditions the organism. Lamarck insists, however, that the organism, while always tending toward the finality of conformation, is the source of all motion. As a result, Lamarck's theory of evolution, far from being reducible to Darwin's attacks, is an attempt to conceptualize a dynamic and temporal relation between the organism and the milieu. Whereas, in the nineteenth century, Auguste Comte's and Hippolyte Taine's philosophical positivism would insist on the determining aspect of the milieu, making human beings mere "products of the environment"[11] (twentieth-century behavioral biology would inherit that adaptionist and creativist tradition),[12] Merleau-Ponty would return in his own way to Lamarck's dynamic intuition. The sociological perspective, which postulates that to be a human being means to be *among* others, and to be shaped by their social milieu, then appears to be related in some way to a more primordial dimension: Being human is being not only *in* a milieu, *amid* a milieu, but rather being *through* a milieu, *via* a milieu. (Note that *parmi,* the French word for "among" or "amid," is derived from the classical Latin *per medio,* "through the medium.")[13]

In following that intuition, Merleau-Ponty will take a particular interest in the psychobiological studies of Jakob von Uexküll and Kurt Goldstein, which establish that biology cannot be modeled on physics: That is, it cannot consider the relation of the organism to its outside in terms of an sheer physical causality. Whereas the relation between the milieu and physical objects is *quantitative,* that between the milieu and its organism is *qualitative.* It is this quality that is missing from behaviorism, which, to borrow Bergson's definition of the comic, "plasters the mechanical onto the living [*plaque de la mécanique sur du vivant*]." Merleau-Ponty will articulate his objections more succinctly in his Sorbonne lectures collected in *Child Psychology and Pedagogy,* which are nothing other than a reformulation of the results of his first two books. Behaviorists believe they can situate themselves within the geographical setting and deduce scientific data from it (*PPE,* 432ff./343ff.). Here Merleau-Ponty is using the distinction, proposed by the Gestalt psychologist Kurt Koffka in his *Principles of Gestalt Psychology,* between "geographical environment" and "behavioral environment."[14] The notion of behavioral environment supposedly proposes a qualitative theory of behavior to counter scientistic behaviorism, but it overlooks *what it is* that behaves, in this case, an organism. It seems, therefore, that Merleau-Ponty's major objection to Koffka's Gestalt psychology would be that it remains trapped within a notion of the environment that— in not taking the dynamism of the organic into account—does not really manage to come up with a theory of the milieu. In other words, Gestalt psychology neglects the dialectic between the living thing and its milieu because it lacks a way of thinking about life.

Two conclusions can be drawn from this analysis of those theories of perception that deem themselves anti-intellectualist, and aren't at all, according to Merleau-Ponty. First, a mechanistic interpretation presupposes an immediate action between the perceived and the perceiving. Its paradigm is the theory of reflexes, which assumes there is a direct transmission from the starting point to the endpoint. Laughter could then be reduced to an electrical stimulation of the facial nerve, as in the experiment of Georges Dumas (*PPE,* 554/446–47). And yet, explains Merleau-Ponty, basing himself on Kurt Goldstein in particular, if there truly is a relation between a stimulus and the response, that relation is not direct: It "necessarily occurs within a milieu: a field of forces" (*PPE*, 433/346). Second, Gestalt psychology attempts to conceptualize the organization of the field and its lines of force by means of the concept of Gestalt, or form. Although Gestalt avoids causalism, according to Merleau-Ponty it quickly loses its roots in perception and tends in the direction of formalism. Even while asserting the coexistence of physical and mental structures, it does not grapple with their complex relation but confines itself to positing a general isomorphism. Where mechanism postulates immediacy, Gestalt psychology espouses the coincidence of structures. In other words, whenever there is a transparency of structures, the Gestalt appears.

Even as he uses the results of mechanism and Gestaltism to refute the classic notions of transparency, Merleau-Ponty maintains that each of them lacks, for reasons of its own, an authentic concept of perception, because the fundamental element is missing: *the living body,* which will be placed at the center of *Phenomenology of Perception.*

From the Milieu to the World

What is a body? Anything we will be able to say about a body, about any body, we will say by the measure of the first body that is given to us as experience: our own. Nevertheless, we have very diverse experiences of that body. We experience it "from the inside," as a sensible, living, moving body, a body we manipulate and by which we act. But that same body can also turn inside out, can become "external" whenever we feel another looking at us. For an instant, we are no longer altogether "in ourselves"; we imagine our bodies perceived by others, an object exposed to an alien gaze. Our bodies become objectified in the experience of being-seen, but also whenever we gaze into a mirror: What we see there "from the outside" never entirely corresponds to what we live "from the inside."

The inherent doubleness of the body was one of Husserl's first intuitions. Since the German language possesses two words where the Latin languages have only one, Husserl distinguishes between the body as object (*Körper*) and the body as subject (*Leib*), living body, *Leib* stemming from the same root as *Leben* (life). Everything seems to indicate, however, that the distinction, fundamental in *Phenomenology of Perception,* became essential for Merleau-Ponty even before he had read Husserl, through contact with the writings of Gabriel Marcel. How to account for the fact that I am a body and that this body is not just any body but rather *my* body? The sentence "I am a body" remains void, so long as we have not realized that *being* a body amounts to *having* a body. That having, however, should not be confused with possessing. In Marcel's 1935 book *Being and Having* (Merleau-Ponty would publish a book review of it the following year),[15] the body thus plays a pivotal role, situated at the crossroads between being and having but also outside that dichotomy. The body "is not," inasmuch as it is never given to me entirely: It will never become an "object."[16] Even though *I have* my body, even though it is the vehicle of my actions, it is never fully accessible to me. *Phenomenology of Perception* can be read as a response to that configuration, which is still all too abstract, since it does not sufficiently account for the fact that *to have* a body is to act not *on* it but *through* it.

The matter at hand, then, is to become conscious that, "for a living being, having a body means being united with a definite milieu, merging with certain projects, and being perpetually engaged therein" (*PP*, 97/84). The perceiving body is always a project(ion), one that is directed, in tension: That is the meaning of the Husserlian notion of intentionality, which Merleau-Ponty will eventually turn into the concept of "motor intentionality" (*intentionnalité motrice*). But what is the body's project, what does it "project"? Not its objects or even really its "intentions"—rather its field, like a projector or even, as Merleau-Ponty explains, a *milieu*. "Insofar as it projects a certain 'milieu' around itself" (*PP*, 269/241), the body is always more than its actuality; it is also and equally in its virtualities.[17] In that sense, the embodied being is not only a being "in a situation," it is defined as a "possibility of situations" (*PP*, 467/431). These possibilities are not only thinkable but concretely realizable, a characteristic that distinguishes them from any transparent thought. "By saying that this intentionality is not a thought, we mean that it is not accomplished in the transparency of a consciousness, and that it takes up as acquired all of the latent knowledge that my body has of itself" (*PP*, 269/241). As a *potentiality in a milieu,* the moving body cannot be reduced to the full autonomy of a pure subject or to the heteronomy of an environment. To grasp its mediacy, therefore, is to allow it to maintain a certain thickness, which it loses in that strange alliance between scientific naturalism and spiritual ontology: "Thus, while the living body became an exterior without an interior, subjectivity became an interior without an exterior, that is, an impartial spectator" (*PP*, 68/56). Whereas *The Structure of Behavior* deliberately begins "from below," *Phenomenology of Perception* situates itself from the start in the human experience of one's own body, which already shifts the perspective. "Human life . . . comprehends itself because it is thrown into a natural world" (*PP*, 377/341, trans. modified). The question of the human thus arises as a problem of the world.[18] Here again, Merleau-Ponty is using Uexküll's studies: The French philosopher's concept of milieu is quite simply the translation of the German term *Umwelt*, which the ethologist takes care to distinguish from *Umgebung* and *Welt*.

Jakob von Uexküll defines the *Umgebung* in terms of its location in an isotropic space, comparable in that respect to Koffka's "geographical environment." Conversely, the *Umwelt* would be a qualitative space corresponding to the "behavioral environment." In conceiving of the *Umwelt* as specific to the living thing, in contrast to the purely geographical *Umgebung,* Uexküll confers a positive meaning on the term; his approach "from below" distinguishes him from Heidegger's privative zoology.[19] Heidegger, starting from the human *Welt,* will in fact conceive of the animal *Umwelt* as necessarily deficient. Whereas for Uexküll, the surrounding world (*Umwelt*)—unlike the *Umgebung*—is already a world, for Heidegger the *Umwelt* is only an impoverished *Welt,* an "un-*Welt.*"[20]

On the question of animality, some have been too quick to see Merleau-Ponty's notion of the world as being derived from Heidegger's. Unlike Heidegger, who believed that recent efforts of zoology to understand the organism in its relation to its environment ultimately remain pointless for philosophy, Merleau-Ponty confirms and extends Kurt Goldstein's and Frederik Buytendijk's analyses of organic life. Contrary to the Heideggerian conceptualization, there would be not so much an encirclement (*Eingenommensein*) and captivation (*Benommenheit*) of the animal by the *Umwelt* as, on the contrary, an *Auseinandersetzung,* an agonal negotiation of an almost Spinozan cast.[21] The organism, far from "always fitting snugly into a determined milieu,"[22] invariably engages with it. There is hardly a fundamental caesura between the animal and human realms, merely a difference in the modality of that engagement. In short, in Merleau-Ponty's conception, the world—in contrast to an inhibitory *Umwelt*—does not comprehend be-ings (*étants*) in the ontological sense of comprehension (understanding, *Verstehen*) but rather comprehends (in the sense of encompassing, enveloping) the potentiality of the milieu. Rather than being dependent on triggers that would be something like the "casing" or "rails" of behavior (*N*, 283/221, trans. modified),[23] human beings maintain a relation of distance, which is always a creative distance. Hence human life "'comprehends' not only some definite milieu, but rather an infinity of possible milieus" (*PP*, 377/341, trans. modified).

It follows that the notion of milieu takes on a new philosophical value in *Phenomenology of Perception,* inasmuch as it is redefined in relation to the body: The body is no longer a "transparent envelope of Spirit" (*PP*, 187/163) but a "means" to make a world out of a milieu (*PP*, 144/125).

Whereas Heidegger sees the *Umwelt* as closure and encirclement, Merleau-Ponty draws from the milieu his conception of openness. Without abandoning the possibility of distinguishing between the animal realm and the human, he makes that distinction not categorical but a matter of degree. Fundamentally, both animals and humans are at once *situated in* a milieu and *open to* it, though human beings potentiate that openness by creating their own worlds. Even while maintaining a division between the animal and the human, Merleau-Ponty explains the development of the latter on the basis of the former; human beings, in using the possibility offered by the condition of openness, liberate themselves from their objective determination.

In the chapter "The Spatiality of One's Own Body and Motility," Merleau-Ponty considers the case history of "Schn." (Schneider is his real name), who cannot manage to visualize himself while he is carrying out an action. A leather worker, he continues to sew and cut leather but is unable to take any distance from himself, to objectify his activity, even less to project himself into different activities. Schneider has merged with his *Umwelt*, the milieu of the leather worker, whose possibilities are limited and univocal: "The normal person reckons with the possible, which thus acquires a sort of actuality without leaving behind its place as a possibility; for the patient, however, the field of the actual is limited to what is encountered in real contact or linked to these givens through an explicit deduction" (*PP*, 127/112). In order for a world to be, a distantiation, a "spacing," must occur: The immediate givens must be broken up, the actual virtualized. For the nonpathological subject, a stimulus is not simply a lever for actualization; it can also give rise to a "virtual movement" anticipating "a certain power for action within the frame of the anatomical apparatus" (*PP*, 126/111). The body of the normal subject thus possesses a faculty of nonactualization, the faculty to "situate itself in the virtual" (ibid., trans. modified). Oddly, then, the act of turning away from the world (ibid.) truly constitutes the condition for a projection of a world. In the course notes collected in *Nature*, Merleau-Ponty will later write: "No longer the body as fusion with an *Umwelt* but rather the body as means or occasion of the projection of a *Welt*" (*N*, 284/222).

It is this transition to a world that Gestalt psychology cannot manage to grasp because it remains prisoner to the idea of an objective world. Inasmuch as it places behavior—as one form among others—*in* the world, it does not take into account the fact that behavior indicates above all the possibility for the *emergence* of a world. In short, Gestalt theory would ultimately locate forms in a physical world and would confine itself to describing the structural correspondence of that world to the representations we make of it. In that sense, it would be a strange alliance between a physicalist presupposition and a critical philosophical procedure. Yet the world, Merleau-Ponty argues, is not, as Kantianism still understood it, a system of a priori relations, it is not "like a crystal cube" that shows "its hidden sides . . . in its present transparency" (*PP*, 378/342). On the contrary, it is an inhabited, invested, and *worked* space, to borrow a term from Hegel that recurs frequently in Merleau-Ponty's writings. When the world's genesis is linked to the milieu, the world cannot be idealized: Like the *Umwelt,* the world "is an intermediate reality between the world such as it exists for an absolute observer and a purely subjective domain" (*N*, 220/167).

In following the notion of milieu throughout Merleau-Ponty's reflections on perception, we have been able to see how his thinking developed by incorporating technical terms to which he assigns new meaning. In placing ourselves outside the domain of philosophy, we are witness to that philosophical revision, the reworking of a term that, far from becoming a rigid concept, remains operative and multiple. The issue at hand is not to remove a notion to the rarefied spheres of the mind but rather to remain in the space between, as Merleau-Ponty concludes in the summary of his philosophical itinerary: "Perhaps these convergent research projects will ultimately bring to light a milieu common to philosophy and to positive science, and will reveal to us, on the near side of the division between subject and pure object, something like a third dimension where our activity and our passivity, our autonomy and our dependency, would cease to be contradictory" (*P2*, 13).

Merleau-Ponty's first phase, then, already participates fully in the effort to avoid reductionism and to consider intermediaries. As a result, milieu is not merely the operative concept that traverses that phase as a common thread; it also points to his philosophical project as such.[24] It is hardly by chance that Merleau-Ponty returns to the concept much later, dedicating many sessions to the milieu in the courses on nature he taught in the late 1950s. By virtue of the notion of *Umwelt,* "the view of the world is not reduced to a sum of exterior events or to a relation to the interior which is not taken in the world" (*N*, 232/177). To understand the role that the milieu plays for animals, Merleau-Ponty continues, one would have to compare it to our dream consciousness, directed toward something that is never seen for itself (*N*, 233/178). The dream could be seen as the prefiguration of a "new notion of the possible" that cannot be reduced to "another eventual occurrence" (*RC*, 137/98). Rather, it would be the place where, in a series of dream images lasting no more than a few seconds, the infinitude of possible links, always remaining in suspense, would take shape. In place of a direct and adequate vision, reveries offer us a vision that, though it hardly allows us to fix phenomena, does provide a glimpse of them. (So too does perception in a state of fatigue, as Peter Handke describes it in his memorable "Essay on Tiredness," which it would be worthwhile to include among the classics of phenomenology.)[25] In opposition to any epistemology of transparency, what is required is a return to behavior within the milieu, to the "*Alltäglichkeit,* [which] is always in the in-between world, always between the lines" (*N*, 268/207, trans. modified). Instead of "trying to squeeze [things] in the pincers of fragmentary events," we must restore the opacity proper to them; we must understand "the organism or the species as mass reality" (*N*, 268–69/207, trans. modified). We would then arrive at an "envelopment-phenomenon . . . which is not to be sought *behind,* but rather *between* the elements" (*N*, 275/213).

That enveloping milieu is less a container than the gap, the distance, that sustains the elements on the inside. It will become the guiding idea not only of the ontology of the visible (as I endeavor to show in chapter 3), but already of the phenomenology of linguistic expression, the second phase in Merleau-Ponty's thought. The hinge between that first inquiry on perception and the reflection on the phenomenon of expression is the critique and reinterpretation of the classic notion of transcendence.

The Problem of Transcendence

"It would be necessary to define transcendental philosophy anew." *The Structure of Behavior* ends with that statement (*SC*, 241/224). It may come as a surprise, given that Merleau-Ponty's approach seems so different from a transcendental enterprise of the Kantian variety. The long succession of examples, the incessant return to the results of the empirical sciences, and the insistence on the prereflexive are all factors that, at first sight, would qualify Merleau-Ponty as a "precritical" philosopher in the sense Kant conferred on that term. But the truth is that Merleau-Ponty not only had the ambition to move beyond critique, he even aspired to reformulate its very principle, namely, the transcendental. In *The Structure of Behavior,* that reworking of the status of the transcendental extends little further than a programmatic sketch, but in *Phenomenology of Perception* he explains the reasons for it even before turning to the analysis of the phenomenal field.

It should be noted, writes Merleau-Ponty in the introduction to his 1945 book, that classic transcendental philosophies first postulate the *necessity* of experience, then seek to establish its conditions of possibility, but at no moment do they reflect the actual event of experiencing (*PP,* 74/61–62). Within such a system, there can be no real exteriority, either as a facticity of perception or in the experience of an Other irreducible to myself. Exteriority is assumed, but it never takes place: The transcendental "I" is anonymous; it is neither in me nor in others. But despite what seems to be an irrevocable condemnation, Merleau-Ponty seeks to save the Kantian project. What he criticizes in Kant is less his transcendental approach than, more precisely, the fact that he did not follow his program—namely, to define cognition in terms of the factual condition of the knowing subject—to its conclusion (*PP*, 255/266). Although Kant clearly saw that there could be no cognition without the intuition of the senses, he introduced the stratum of the *a priori*, which, though not chronologically antecedent, is logically so.[26] Inasmuch as "the *a priori* maintains its character in Kant's philosophy of that which ought to be the case, in opposition to what exists in fact and as an anthropological determination," he introduces a hierarchy between "what the world ought to be and what the world actually is" (*PP*, 255/266). And that hierarchy leads him to fall short of his own objective. "If a world is to be possible . . .": In that expression, which recurs several times in Kant's writings, the rational subject is not only placed in a position that is in some sense *prior to* the world, the subject also becomes its lawmaker as it were, since the subject posits the conditions for the world's genesis (*PrP*, 50/16–17). The heterogeneity between the transcendental aesthetic on the one hand and the transcendental analytic on the other cannot be resolved—still according to Merleau-Ponty—except by conferring on the subject the status of a God who posits the world, not that of a human who "is attached to it" (*PP*, 254/228). In the last instance, that amounts to reintroducing dogmatism into a critical philosophy that purports to be free of it. Only in appearance would such a philosophy of the constituting subject be the antithesis of the naturalistic view that the world is populated by constituted objects: Together they are only the twofold aspect that the prejudice "of a universe perfectly explicit in itself" can assume (*PP*, 51/44). The only difference is that, in the transcendental version, the de facto condition is combined with a de jure condition: In short, the explanation *must* be possible and consequently must already be "completed somewhere" (*PP*, 74/62).

That line of argument, which had a considerable impact on French phenomenology,[27] remains somewhat hasty, however. To grasp its import, we need to take a detour through Merleau-Ponty's sources: Husserl and Sartre, of course, but also and especially Eugen Fink. Before Merleau-Ponty, Husserl had criticized Kant for the idea of a law inscribed before the fact. Transcendental philosophy is thereby reduced to a "regressive inquiry" that wonders "in what conceptual and legal forms [*Begriffs- und Gesetzformen*] an objective world in general (a world of nature) must present itself."[28] In his effort to demarcate his own transcendental philosophy from that of his predecessor, Husserl judges that, for Kant, the idea of the transcendental is still confined to a "scientistic" framework consisting solely of the laws of nature. Husserl, by contrast, believes that this framework must be "broadened" to take into account "the multiple forms of human societies and the cultural products originating in the life of the community," inasmuch as they too configure the experiences possible.[29] Transcendental phenomenology is thus the description of intentional consciousness. That consciousness, much more than a mere condition a priori, would be something quite real, directed toward life and its "concrete *plenitude*."[30]

And yet in *The Transcendence of the Ego* (1934), which we know Merleau-Ponty had read attentively, Sartre warned all who, on the pretext of wanting to correct Kant's critical philosophy, sought to "*realize*"—that is, to give factual reality to—what was in Kantian thought merely a simple form of understanding. In his "transcendental turn," therefore, Husserl would have reified the transcendental into an ego in which consciousness is situated: "Thus transcendental consciousness becomes thoroughly personal."[31] In that way, Husserl supposedly "weighed down" consciousness and—Sartre is playing on words here—in making it "ponderous," he also made it "ponderable."[32]

According to Sartre, however, the transcendental consciousness must be entirely purified of the ego, which would still be an alien element installed within it. Consciousness must be conceived as "clear and lucid" through and through: "The object with its characteristic opacity is before consciousness, but consciousness is purely and simply consciousness of being consciousness of that object."[33] There is thus no place for an "I" that would inevitably become an "occupant" surpassing the limits of mere consciousness, an object *for* that consciousness, which for that reason will never be able to be a subject *of* that consciousness. As a result, the transcendental field is inevitably a "pre-personal" agency and the precondition for any empirical "I." Purified of any egological structure, consciousness recovers its initial "limpid density": In order to be able to welcome the *whole*, it must be conceived as *nothingness*.[34] With that interpretation of transcendental phenomenology, Sartre is notably in conflict with the reading Eugen Fink gives of it in his article "The Phenomenological Philosophy of Edmund Husserl and Contemporary Criticism," which Sartre twice quotes.

In that essay, which appeared in *Kant-Studien* in 1933 and which influenced Merleau-Ponty very early on,[35] Husserl's last assistant tried to separate the use of the word "transcendental" in phenomenology from the sense neo-Kantianism was giving it at the time. The error committed by Husserlian critical hermeneutics would supposedly consist of applying to Husserl its own conceptual grids. Although beginning in 1906 Husserl used a somewhat Kantian terminology, he took care to distinguish the meaning he was giving to the terms he borrowed. According to Fink, one has to understand that, unlike in Kantian thought, for Husserl the transcendental ego is an individual and existing ego. Instead of contrasting an empirical self to a nonempirical transcendental subject, one would have to distinguish between an empirical ego, the object of a worldly apperception, and a transcendental ego, which is deprived of that apperception but is nonetheless a be-ing.[36] That "constituting entity" (*être constituant*) is both less and more than the Kantian subject: *less,* because, in the correlation with the world, the form of subjectivity has no priority over the be-ings of the world qua possible objects of cognition; *more,* because consciousness is not only that which contains within itself the form of any possible cognition but also the very site of the constitution of the world. But the specific question of the being of that constituting entity is left hanging. Fink, even while presenting himself as the defender of Husserlian philosophy closest to its author's will, has undeniably already added on his own thinking, strongly influenced by that of Heidegger. Like Heidegger (and unlike Sartre), Fink believes that what is at stake in the transcendental must be formulated not on the basis of a pure consciousness but on the basis of the facticity of the being engaged in the world. Although Husserl, with respect to Kantian epistemological laws, truly brought about a revolution by asking the question of *constitution,* "the question of the mode of being [*Seinsart*] of what does the constituting"—as Heidegger insinuates in his famous 1927 letter to Husserl.[37]

These issues, which are echoed in Eugen Fink's and Ludwig Landgrebe's subsequent texts of 1939, which Merleau-Ponty read immediately after his visit to Leuven,[38] did not fail to give rise to reflections on his part. Husserl, of course, could do no more than dismiss flat out the Heideggerian criticisms, since in his eyes the operation of the transcendental reduction brought to light only the being of the constituting entity. In *Phenomenology of Perception,* Merleau-Ponty indicates, however, that phenomenology so conceived is barely distinguishable from intellectualism, or worse, psychologism: "This new 'reduction' could thus know but one true subject, namely the meditating Ego. This passage from the created [*nature*] to the creating [*naturant*], or from the constituted to the constituting, would complete the thematization begun by psychology and would no longer leave anything implicit or implied in my knowledge" (*PP*, 73/61). And he adds that "such is the standard perspective of a transcendental philosophy as well as, at least in appearance, the program of a transcendental phenomenology" (*PP*, 73/61). But, asks Merleau-Ponty, what remains of the phenomenological in such a philosophy? If the description of the lifeworld (*Lebenswelt*) is only a propaedeutic, destined to be replaced by a transcendental reflection "where all of the obscurities of the world would be clarified," "it would not be clear why reflection would have to pass through the lifeworld" (*PP*, 419n1/553n14, trans. modified). But then what is an authentically phenomenological notion of the transcendental? Without a transcendental subject and on the basis of a description of intentional life experiences, can one still develop a philosophy that deserves the name "transcendental"? The Sartrian thesis of consciousness as a "prepersonal" agency would in any case provide an alternative to Husserlian subjectivism. But, Merleau-Ponty believes (*PP*, 320n/544n60), if one displaces agency away from the "I," in order to make it a "relative and pre-personal" "I," one pretends to resolve the aporia when in reality it only becomes more solidly entrenched. In his endeavor to abandon the idea of an ego that would be *in front of* the world, Sartre's "nothingness" of consciousness is reduced to a container-milieu from which one can then draw an inventory, at will.

Along with Fink, Merleau-Ponty thinks that, on the contrary, we must conceive of the transcendental subject as a be-ing among be-ings, as intra-ontic being. Although transcendental reduction is imaginable, it can hardly be conceived in terms of the model of an ultimate ground that would have to be reached. Rather, it is to be seen as an interminable exercise that, through the modification of being—and thus of be-ings—makes it possible to glimpse a common ground that is never possessed. While he was reading Fink, Merleau-Ponty also discovered in Leuven Husserl's fragment "The Earth Doesn't Move" for *The Crisis of European Sciences*, a fragment that gave new coherence to that idea. Husserl says that, in response to the Copernican and Galilean revolutions, against which Kantian thought can be measured, he is starting a counterrevolution. In this text, which is also known as "The Overthrow of Copernican Theory" ("Umsturz der kopernikanischen Lehre"),[39] Merleau-Ponty believes he can detect the archetype for another "transcendental ground," at the opposite extreme of the early Husserl's logicism. The Earth, he paraphrases, "is not in motion like objective bodies, but not at rest either, since we cannot see what it could be 'tacked on' to" (*SG*, 227/180). As "soil" or "stem," it would prefigure a new idea of the sensible foundation "of our thought as it is of our life" (ibid.). Even before there can be a transcendental philosophy, empirical experience is necessary: "As Kant himself said profoundly," Merleau-Ponty writes in "The Primacy of Perception," "we can only think the world because we have already experienced it" (*PrP*, 50/17). Kant's error was to have wanted to seek a ground more solid than the uncertain ground of the world of the senses, which, however, is the only one available to us. To rethink the transcendental, the issue raised at the end of *The Structure of Behavior*, is therefore simply to become conscious that, after all, the world may be the transcendental condition of the transcendental itself—if, that is, that hyperbole still has any meaning.

"Along with the natural world and the social world," Merleau-Ponty concludes, "we have discovered that which is truly transcendental, which is not the collection of constitutive operations through which a transparent world, without shadows and without opacity, is spread out in front of an impartial spectator, but rather the ambiguous life where the *Ursprung* of transcendences takes place, which, through a fundamental contradiction, puts me into communication and on this basis makes knowledge possible" (*PP*, 418–19/382). As such, that transcendental is literally a condition of *possibility*. Merleau-Ponty insists on that last term: The field, insofar as it is limited but nevertheless unenclosable, allows for variation; as "principle of indetermination" (*PP*, 197/172), it opens the possibility of another oriented attitude (the Husserlian concept of *Einstellung*) against the backdrop of a world characterized as horizontality.[40]

What interests Merleau-Ponty in the notion of transcendence is not so much a new notion of foundation (like Husserl in his transcendental idealist phase) as the act of transcending. (In that way, Merleau-Ponty paradoxically returns to the near side of the rigorous distinction, dating back at least to Kant's *Critique of Pure Reason,* between the *transcendent* as a precritical dogmatic principle and the *transcendental* as an epistemological condition of critical philosophy.) Yet the matter at hand is not to move out of the world but to move permanently toward what is not yet possessed within the world, as Eugen Fink's 1933 article suggested.[41] The opacity of the world is correlated to and inseparable from an "*active* transcendence" (*PP*, 431/395), an "ek-stase" of the subject "oriented or polarized toward what he is not" (*PP*, 491/454), an "act of transcendence by which the subject opens himself to the natural world and carries himself along" (*PP*, 180/191, trans. modified), rather reminiscent of Ernst Bloch's "transcending without transcendence."

We would therefore have to see that reflection on apriority less as a critique actually directed at Kant (Merleau-Ponty grafts his own inquiries onto Kantian terminology) than as an indicator of a general movement. Undeniably—and despite the emphasis on inherence in a world-milieu—*Phenomenology of Perception* truly constitutes an effort to conceptualize the activity of the subjective pole. When the subject is collapsed to its corporeal condition alone, there is no longer any possibility of explaining how one moves beyond oneself—a point to which *The Visible and the Invisible* will return. The notion of a transcendental movement is still present in the uncompleted work, though Merleau-Ponty explains that that movement beyond cannot be conceived as a movement "by oneself,"[42] only as a "mute transcendence" accompanying phenomenality itself. The field in which Merleau-Ponty finds, first, the marker for an active transcendence—which he attempts to describe as "ex-pression"—and then the milieu for an anonymization that dissolves the residue of a philosophy of consciousness and leads toward an ontology of the sensible, is the field of language.

2

Language

Expression

At the top of the hierarchy of *The Structure of Behavior* stands symbolic behavior. Merleau-Ponty does not say that symbolic behavior *has* a meaning; more exactly, it *is* already meaning through and through. *Phenomenology of Perception* will take up at the precise spot where this first book ends, particularly in its sixth chapter, "The Body as Expression, and Speech." Spelling out the assertion implied by the title, it elaborates on the relationship between the "body" (*corps propre*) and "expression." In some sense, *The Structure of Behavior* already represents a sketch for the later philosophical revision of the notion of behavior.[1] That attempt to move beyond the biological by means of symbolic behavior is then fully developed in the analysis of the body's signifying power in *Phenomenology of Perception*. Merleau-Ponty argues that "the use that a man makes of his body is transcendent with regard to that body as a mere biological being" (*PP*, 220/195). Hence, whenever the *Leib* seizes on existence, there is already an "act of transcendence," an act that "is initially found in the acquisition of a behavior and then in the silent communication of the gesture" (*PP*, 226/199). This act leads to articulate language. Each time, in that taking up and seizing of the world (ibid.), the body is "the place or, rather, the very actuality of the phenomenon of expression" (*PP*, 171/244); more precisely, it represents the "very movement of expression" (*PP*, 171/147). Whereas in *The Structure of Behavior* Merleau-Ponty marked his distance

from any intellectualist approach to the relationship between consciousness and nature, choosing to enter into dialogue with the empirical disciplines rather than with philosophical doctrines, he now attempts to reinsert
the problem of idealization into behavior itself to avoid the split between
the two spheres, which would only shore up intellectualism. In speech there
is truly an act, but "speech can be said to be neither an 'intellectual operation' nor a 'motor phenomenon': it is entirely motricity and entirely intelligence" (*PP*, 227/200).

These terms are at first sight somewhat puzzling. By all appearances,
Merleau-Ponty is not simply criticizing a static model of language and replacing it with a mobile model. Although there is a signifying act, there is
no instrumental "intellectual operation," no willful, "doing" subject. Conversely, language cannot be reduced to pure passivity, to a motor phenomenon in the sense of being moved or driven. These two notions—one
intellectualist, the other naturalistic—turn out to be two versions of the
self-same operationalism.[2] Between an approach that would see language
as the operation of translating an idea and one in which every act of speech
is only a realization of a linguistic schema, Merleau-Ponty places himself
within the perspective of a language in the making, an act of speech "in a
nascent state" (*PP*, 229/202). For this reason, it seems only logical that
Merleau-Ponty would seek in expressive speech—particularly literary
speech—a positive example as a means to move beyond his timeworn
schema of double negation (neither . . . nor). To achieve this, he estab-
lishes a close correlation between speech and body, conceiving of linguistic
expression as a potentialization of the motility inherent in the body.
Nevertheless—and once again, this can be seen as the fundamental ambiva-
lence still pervasive in *Phenomenology of Perception*—though expression
is not the expression of an idea, it remains irremediably the expression of a
consciousness. In his attempt to mitigate the split between consciousness
and body, Merleau-Ponty goes so far as to establish, through the notion of
intentional motility, a continuity between consciousness, the body, and
expression. The notion of motility, while emphasizing the importance of
perception at the expense of a "guiding idea," also indicates—in *Phenomenology of Perception*—a modality of seizing the world. Through the body
("means" and "instrument"), consciousness expresses not "I think therefore I am" but rather "I am because I can" (*PP*, 160/139).

For sure, the idea of intentional motility or rather motor intentionality
(*intentionnalité motrice*) moves away from the classical cognitive model of
intentionality toward a conception of intentionality as a *dynamic capacity*.
Yet in this first phase of Merleau-Ponty's work, this dynamic capacity is
clearly still attributed to an authoritative instance: the subject. Instead of

conceiving of bodily behavior as a reaction to external stimuli, behavior is now defined as symbolic, that is, as the expression of an intentional movement that transcends its mere physical or physiological function. In short, while the move toward expressive behavior rebukes both the naturalistic determinism and the cognitivist internalism, the dynamic of the movement keeps a clear origin: the subject that "ex-presses" itself through embodied practices. For Merleau-Ponty, to exist bodily means more than just the assurance to *be*; it means to have a capacity to move beyond what one currently holds onto, to have the *power* of reaching beyond one's own reach. Paradoxically, thus this ek-static decentering of the self ultimately leads to reinforcing its priority, when *Phenomenology of Perception*, insofar as it remains fundamentally subservient to the model of an active subjective pole, comes to interpret the potentiality of expression as the capacity of a subjective I.[3]

It would seem that Merleau-Ponty himself became aware of the aporias in which an approach that affirms the continuity of consciousness, body, and expression is enmeshed and that he attempted to establish expression as such on an antepredicative emotional base. Interestingly, one of the hypotheses that can be put forward to explain the theoretical shift during the "middle period," between 1945 and the early 1950s, is that, by trying to give an account of the phenomenon of expression, Merleau-Ponty came to reconsider the Husserlian problem of ideality, which he had largely left aside in *Phenomenology of Perception*. This is all the more surprising in that, initially, Merleau-Ponty's focus is not so much on the *permanence* of a specific meaning (its ideality) but on its *event*. What are the conditions that have to be met in order for expression to occur? True expression, as he had already said in *Phenomenology of Perception*, must be creative: "Expression is everywhere creative, and what is expressed is always inseparable from it" (*PP*, 448/391). But if that is the case, expression is pervaded by an almost insurmountable paradox, between the demand for fidelity and the demand for creativity. Expression needs to be faithful to that which it expresses; at the same time it needs to reinterpret it in a new way in order to meet the demands of creativity. If to express something is to bring to the fore (*ex-primere*) a given meaning and confer on it a new form, then the very event of expression inevitably contaminates and modifies what is to be expressed. A truly faithful translation would have to refrain altogether from searching for a new form; it would amount to a translation without the act of translation, a content in its pristine state, devoid of any contaminating external form, so to speak. Conversely, a purely creative event that would not be determined in any way by a preexisting meaning would be simply form without content, mere gesticulation. In a way, expression brings to the fore something that did not exist before the act of expression but was quite simply created by it. At the same time, however, there is a kind of retrospective illusion that what was to be expressed was simply there, waiting to be brought to our attention. Expression tends to produce what Bergson dubbed the "retrograde movement of the true," where, starting from a moment in the present, one retroactively invents the conditions that may have made it possible. As Merleau-Ponty says, expression always "antedates itself" (*EP*, 35/29).

As it were, expression has to grapple with two (impossible) extremes: that of being a purely creative act and that of being a purely repetitive act. Whence the *paradox of* expression: Although a thoroughly creative discourse would say nothing, a merely repetitive discourse would have nothing to say.[4] It is quite clear that this means that the phenomenon of expression cannot be traced back to any of its preceding elements, since it consists in their integration (in the mathematical sense of the word). As a result, the event of expression (the "saying") is irreducible not only to the order of the expressed (the "said") but also to that of the speaker. This might be one reason that Merleau-Ponty came to be increasingly aware of the contradictions that arise when trying to deduce the discursive from the gestural.[5] Indeed, if intellectualism overlooks the expressive act by reducing language to dimensions that are purely ideal, an approach that deliberately restricts itself to describing the act of expression as gesture is inevitably led to overlook the ideality proper to language. Although the shift from reflex behavior to symbolic behavior can be glimpsed in the description of "phonetic gesticulation" (*PP*, 211/186), that description can account only for the most rudimentary, the most recurrent, and as a result the most predictable forms of communication. And yet the aspect of language that Merleau-Ponty embraces above all, and which impels him to grant it increasingly more attention, is its properly creative aspect, its potentiality for ideation.

So long as one remains within an explanation of language as "motor potentiality" (*PP*, 462/425, trans. modified), one necessarily overlooks the *intelligence* proper to language. In wanting at all cost to counter the "bird's-eye view" of intellectualism (*PM*, 24/15) with an approach "from below" that considers language a superior form of original motility, Merleau-Ponty cannot account for the ideality inherent in all language. He multiplies examples of anti-intellectualist gestures, such as the expression of anger or the act of smiling, to which he appeals to mark the indifferentiation between the idea and its expression. Nevertheless, he already seems to realize that this "emotivist" theory, in which what is externalized is only an immediate translation not yet marred by the symbolic and cultural mediations of an internal state,[6] cannot explain the communication occurring in conventional systems, which, though resting on a "keyboard of acquired significations" (*PP*, 217/192), like musical performance, allows for an infinite variation of new significations, precisely through the difference between signifier and signified.

The architecture of *Phenomenology of Perception* leaves no doubt: The problem of language is still subordinated to the more general problem of expression. In addition to linguistic expression, it encompasses the gestural, the musical, the pictorial, and other forms. At the same time, expression is considered solely from the perspective of the somatic moving beyond itself. That explains the absolute rejection of any linguistics that posits the arbitrary or conventional character of language. The syntax of a language, its declensions, rules of conjugation, and prosody are less the translation of an "arbitrary convention" than a way "for the human body to celebrate the world and finally to experience it" (*PP*, 218/193, trans. modified). In short, the problem of language is never considered outside the perspective of the expressive body. Within that viewpoint, then, "there are, strictly speaking, no conventional signs" (*PP*, 219/194). Language would not be the mirror of an abstract cogitation, a "simple notation of a thought that is pure and clear for itself" (ibid.), but rather a turmoil that arises amid the thickness of the living body. Between the lines of this chapter, "The Body as Expression, and Speech," can be discerned a harsh judgment of any purely formal linguistics that would believe it could eliminate the fleshly character of signs in the hope of reaching a state of "transparency" or "clarity of language." If there is truly a primordial language, it would have to be sought rather "in emotional gesticulation" (ibid.).

There is reason to wonder, however, whether that does not overlook the most important aspect of a conventionalist approach, one that breaks the bond between signifier and signified, and whether Merleau-Ponty's critique of transparency does not apply above all to his own conception. In its overemphasis on the corporeal envelope, the emotivist theory—despite a few concessions to cultural relativity here and there[7]—tends to make meaning and the expression of meaning converge toward a state of indistinction. Merleau-Ponty, criticizing an externalist approach, refused to limit the difference between the expression of anger or love to a difference in outward gesticulations (which could then be explained in terms of a cultural conventionalism). He instead located it in "a difference between the emotions themselves" (*PP*, 220/195).[8] The author of *Phenomenology of Perception* tirelessly repeated that the inaugural act by which any meaning is established must be rediscovered under the sedimented and instituted layers of meaning: "Our view of man will remain superficial so long as we do not return to this origin, so long as we do not rediscover the primordial silence beneath the noise of words, and so long as we do not describe the gesture that breaks this silence" (*PP*, 214/190). And he adds: "Speech is a gesture, and its signification is a world" (ibid.). Conventionalism is rejected outright in favor of a gestural theory of language (*PP*, 218/193), a view that also implies that every gesture produces its own world.

The consequences are only too obvious. The critique of transparency, here deployed vis-à-vis language, does not culminate in a challenge to intellectualism; rather, that challenge forms the basis for a different type of transparency, this time between what is to be expressed and its expression. There is a risk, when the event of expression is too deeply rooted in a sensible body from which it is supposed to emerge, that its status will be predetermined, even though, according to Merleau-Ponty, the matter at hand is precisely to understand its meaning. Meaning is not in things, nor is it established by a symbolic gesture resembling that of Adamic naming; it does not belong to the speaking subject, nor is it derived from the signified. Rather, it always stands at a remove. The meaning of language, then, cannot be reduced to movement or to thought: It obeys an immanent logic, and the language event is intralinguistic.

This fact undoubtedly explains why Merleau-Ponty will detach the problem of language from his previous investigations and will devote the majority of his time to it in the following years, even reaching the point of claiming that the problem of language "contains all the others, including the problem of philosophy" (*SG*, 116/93). "The problem of philosophy" would thus be to describe the emergence of meaning without reducing it to the transparency of the signified or limiting it to the signs in and through which it appears, that is, without materializing or spiritualizing it (*PPE*, 84/64). In his courses at the Sorbonne, Merleau-Ponty expressed the problem in these terms: "This mediation of the objective and the subjective, the interior and the exterior, what philosophy searches for, we can find in language if we succeed in approaching it closely" (*PPE*, 87/67, trans. modified).

In the years following the publication of *Phenomenology of Perception*, Merleau-Ponty made frequent reference to works in the field of linguistics, a discipline that by definition envisions language as independent from its singular embodiments. This is a sign of the attention he was beginning to pay to the scientific study of language. In order to explain the turn that occurred in the years following the publication of *Phenomenology of Perception*, commentators have for the most part considered the later texts, those written between 1959 and 1961, largely underestimating the importance of what had taken place between 1945 and 1952, namely, Merleau-Ponty's election to the Collège de France. Although the philological evidence is still sketchy,[9] a mere glance at Merleau-Ponty course titles gives us insight into his preoccupations. In Lyon, he dedicated a 1947–48 course to "Language and Communication," and the announcement of the course he was to teach at the École Normale Supérieure in 1948 reads simply "Saussure." A year later, he taught a class titled "Consciousness and the Acquisition of Language" at the Sorbonne, and immediately afterward, if we are to believe Claude Lefort's preface, began work on the manuscript that would be published posthumously as *The Prose of the World* (1964). At the first "Colloque international de phénomenologie" in Royaumont in 1951, Merleau-Ponty's topic was the phenomenology of language.

To gauge that increased interest in linguistics, still absent from *Phenomenology of Perception* or reduced to caricature, we must turn to the special issue on Edmund Husserl of the *Revue Internationale de Philosophie* (1939), which we know Merleau-Ponty read very carefully. Among other articles (by Banfi, Fink, Hering, Landgrebe, and Patočka, among others) that ultimately convinced Merleau-Ponty of the usefulness of a systematic study of phenomenology, the one by the Dutch linguist H. J. Pos established a link between Husserlian inquiries and recent advances in the linguistic sciences.[10] In his 1947 essay "The Metaphysical in Man" (*SNS*, 102–19/83–98), Merleau-Ponty observes that the "revision of the subject-object relation" pervading the human sciences was particularly evident in recent works on linguistics (*SNS*, 106/86). He mentions Antoine Meillet, Walther von Wartburg, and especially Gustave Guillaume. Later manuscripts would consider Joseph Vendryès and Karl Bühler, Roman Jakobson, Nikolai Trubetzkoy, and the Prague Linguistic Circle in general, but also psycholinguistics, to which the child psychology courses of 1949–52 make abundant reference.[11] Paul Ricoeur's judgment that Merleau-Ponty "rushes past the objective science of signs" because he does not make the "long detour by way of linguistics"[12] therefore proves to be hasty.

Although Merleau-Ponty demonstrated an intense interest in the linguistics of his time, there was one linguist who, more than all the others, brought about a profound "upheaval" in the philosopher's thinking: Ferdinand de Saussure.[13] Roland Barthes rightly points out that Merleau-Ponty was the first to introduce the Genevan linguist into philosophy,[14] though it would be more accurate to speak of "use" rather than of a proper, didactic introduction. As is his habit, Merleau-Ponty does not read Saussure as a philologist would but rather takes him as the ground and fertilizer for his own reflections. He weaves together a text in which—in the words of "The Philosopher and His Shadow" regarding productive exegesis—the one "we are speaking about and the one who is speaking are present together, although it is not possible even in principle to decide at any given moment just what belongs to each" (*EP*, 200/159, trans. modified).[15]

The Specter of a Pure Language

"What we have learned from Saussure," begins the essay "Indirect Language and the Voices of Silence" (*SG*, 49/39), is that, "taken singly, signs do not signify anything and that each of them does not so much express a meaning as mark a divergence of meaning between itself and other signs." If we look closely at that assertion, we find it entails two theses: First, signifying units are not merely the reverberation of things that exist before language; and second, they do not contain an intrinsic meaning in themselves. That dual thesis takes on two myths threatening to ensnare any emphatic theory of language haunted by the "specter of a pure language." In the chapter by that title, which constitutes the first part of *The Prose of the World*, Merleau-Ponty returns to the ideal "we all secretly venerate . . . a language which in the last analysis would deliver us from language by delivering us to things" (*PM*, 8/4). We would all be modern Cratyluses, fantasizing, without admitting it to ourselves, about a "prehistoric language spoken in things," dreaming nostalgically of a "golden age of language in which words once adhered to the objects themselves" (*PM*, 12/6). It is to that age, it should be recalled, that Michel Foucault would dedicate the first chapter of *The Order of Things*, called precisely (and how can it be a coincidence?) "The Prose of the World." Unfortunately, that "myth of a language of things" (*PM*, 12/7) partakes of the "magical belief which puts the word 'sun' in the center of the sun" (*PM*, 10/5) and cannot stand up against the arguments of an ancient or modern Hermogenes.

Another myth threatens to ensnare us, one that seems contrary to the first but which is only its "sublimated form": the chimera of a "universal language" (*PM*, 12/7, trans. modified). Under the cover of a rational approach, philosophical reflections on language have often taken the form of an archaeology of the linguistic a priori. In several places, Merleau-Ponty mentions the project of the early Husserl, who, on the model of a "pure logic," envisions establishing the rules of a "pure grammar" onto which every empirical language could be graphed. The philosopher and grammarian, we read in the *Logical Investigations*, "must lay bare an ideal framework which each actual language will fill up and clothe differently, in deference . . . to empirical motives,"[16] and this *grammaire générale et raisonnée* (in French in the text!) would then make it possible to determine how "German, Latin, Chinese express 'the' existential proposition, 'the' categorical proposition, 'the' antecedent of a hypothetical, 'the' plural, 'the' modalities of possibility and probability, 'the' negative, etc."[17] And yet, Merleau-Ponty comments, Husserl forgets that "to achieve a universal grammar it is not enough to leave Latin grammar, and that the list of the possible forms of signification which he gives bears the mark of the language which he himself spoke" (*PM*, 38/26). Instead of reproaching Husserl, as Anton Marty had done upon the publication of *Logical Investigations* in 1900/1901, for confusing the a priori and the empirical, Merleau-Ponty seeks to demonstrate the incongruity of a theory postulating a "language without words" (*PM*, 24/16). Writers themselves, generally little inclined toward intellectualist constructions, are not safe from the myth of a reign of pure meaning. Merleau-Ponty is surprised, for example, by a passage in which the seventeenth-century French moralist La Bruyère claims he needs to find the exact, unique, and irreplaceable word that can convey his thought (*PM*, 11/6). In that view, all that would be required of the writer would be "to meet the phrase ready made in the limbo of language, to recover the muted language in which being murmurs to us" (ibid., trans. modified). In a strange, unavowed alliance, such an idea of literature— which often becomes a "fixed belief" (ibid.)—comes to coincide with the representations of intellectualism.

With the benefit of a certain distance, two major articulations of an ideology of the transparency of language seem to be taking shape: In the first, the sign corresponds to the object; in the second, it coincides with signification.[18] To work against these two myths, Saussurean linguistics advances two apposite concepts: the idea of the *arbitrariness* of the sign and that of its *differential* character.

Saussure's notion of *arbitrariness* breaks with the naturalistic explanation of language. The linguistic sign maintains no causal link to natural objects or to the phonic substance: It depends on an *institution* of meaning.[19] The use of the scholastic notion of phonic *substance* should not mislead us: Speech is called a "substance" because it is the union of one or several phonemes with a concrete meaning. And though speech is certainly the necessary support for any linguistic actualization, its link to virtual form (language) is purely arbitrary. Saussure insists, however, that though the institution of signification is arbitrary, that does not mean it depends on the will of the speaking subject. And Merleau-Ponty will no doubt revise the judgment he had made of arbitrariness in *Phenomenology of Perception* on the basis of this remark. The term "arbitrary," the *Course on General Linguistics* cautions, "should not imply that the choice of the signifier is left entirely to the speaker."[20] By *arbitrary*, Saussure adds, "I mean that it is unmotivated, i.e. arbitrary in that it actually has no natural connection with the signified."[21]

The sign, though having no natural connection to its outside, does maintain connections of a different sort. Marked by an essential poverty, it acquires its meaning only by its position in a constellation of signs to which it belongs. If we are to avoid the impasse of something like a totally self-enclosed, autarkic sign, its *arbitrary* character must be associated with its inevitable counterpart, namely, its *differential* character. Instead of a meaning intrinsic to the sign, what takes shape is a shifting and oppositional structure, where the relationship between signifier and signified is played out in different times and cultures, along with the capacity to synthesize and differentiate what is being signified. For example, some languages distinguish between two signifieds when designating a child, depending on whether it is male or female (*puer* and *puella* in Latin, *bambino* and *bambina* in Italian), while others perceive only a single signified (the Greek *teknon* or the Neapolitan *criatura*).[22] That is because, as Merleau-Ponty explains in the chapter "Science and the Experience of Expression," "to speak is not to have at one's disposal a certain number of signs . . . [but] to possess language as a principle of distinction" (*PM*, 46/32, trans. modified). And he again borrows a Saussurean example: "There are languages in which one cannot say 'to sit in the sun,' because they use particular words to refer to the rays of sunlight and keep the word 'sun' for the star itself" (ibid.).

It turns out, then, that perception of the world is dependent on the way language carves up the vast set of signifieds, but also on how it overlaps and reshapes them. Our vision would be, if not determined, then at least strongly influenced by these fault lines that map language's topology. That limitation is not a hindrance, however, but the very condition for communication. "This miracle that a finite number of signs, forms, and words should give rise to an indefinite number of uses . . . is the very genius of speech, and anyone who tries to explain it in terms of its 'beginning' or its 'end' would lose sight of its 'doing'" (*PM*, 59/41, trans. modified). In that sense, "the power of language lies neither in that future of knowledge toward which it moves nor in that mythical past from which it has emerged" (*PM*, 58/41). Rather, it is located entirely in the place where "language works," in the Wittgensteinian sense.

At the Royaumont conference in 1958, where prominent Continental and Anglo-American analytic philosophers met for the first time, Merleau-Ponty saw a real convergence between Gilbert Ryle's post-Wittgensteinian philosophy and his own phenomenological project, even beyond Ryle's reading of phenomenology. In reply to Ryle's paper, he noted: "In addition to this conceptual content that one can try to give words, in language they do a type of work. The work of a term such as 'if,' for example, might not be rendered by a conceptual analysis of the term 'if.' And, along with Wittgenstein, [Ryle] showed the possibility of a type of clarification of these terms which is not a description of objects" (*PACR*, 93–94/66). Pursuing the idea of an *open pragmatics* of language, Merleau-Ponty would thus return to Wilhelm von Humboldt's suggestion that language cannot be considered a made work (*ergon*) but must be described as an activity, a making of itself (*energeia*).

Merleau-Ponty also borrows from Humboldt the idea of a linguistic "totality" or "universe," which he thinks must also apply to Saussure's theory. "In sum, we have found that signs, morphemes, and words, taken one by one, signify nothing; they succeed in conveying signification only through their assembly; and in the end, communication passes from the totality of spoken language to the totality of heard language" (*PM*, 59/42, trans. modified). It is clear that Merleau-Ponty, in forging that surprising alliance between Humboldt and Saussure—which Saussure would no doubt have rejected—in the last instance looks at the two authors through what could be called a "Gestaltist" lens, retaining only their vision of language as a totality. "A language is less a sum of signs," we read in *The Prose of the World*, "than a methodical means of discriminating signs from one another and thereby constructing a linguistic universe" (*PM*, 45/31).

The manuscripts of *The Prose of the World* clearly convey Merleau-Ponty's desire to take hold of both ends of the chain, a desire that was never abandoned and is undoubtedly the most accurate way to characterize his thought. For him, attention to language and a fortiori to reiteration, made possible by the finite quality of the elements that compose the signifying code, must never come at the expense of the perceptual and somatic dimension. A marginal note indicates (in opposition to the thesis put forward by the linguist Joseph Vendryès) that there is no pure structure of language: "These limits and values exist; quite simply, they are of a perceptual order: there is a *Gestalt* of language" (*PM*, 53/37). Can Gestalt psychology's discovery of the relationship between figure and ground pave the way for a more general determination of meaning relationships as a reciprocal differentiation of elements, but without renouncing their sensible foundation? In other words, can the sensible itself be conceived as a common fabric on which the relationship between an appearing meaning and an inapparent ground are constantly being refigured? In Merleau-Ponty's writings, Saussure's purely structural notion of the "diacritical" will acquire the value of a perceptible interval forming a pattern on the sensible fabric itself. If we remember that *aisthèsis* used to be the name the Greeks gave to the sensible access to the world, it will then be possible to speak of an *aesthetics of intervals,* on the model of Aby Warburg's "iconology of intervals."

The Diacritical

Saussure taught us that every sign "does not so much express a meaning as mark a divergence of meaning between itself and other signs" (*SG*, 49/39), and that divergence is precisely what is concealed in our everyday consciousness of language. Merleau-Ponty, in describing the sort of speech he calls "speaking speech," as opposed to an already sedimented "spoken speech," will thus highlight the inventive, creative, and institutive function of expression. Expression "does not simply choose a sign for an already defined signification, the way one searches for a hammer to drive in a nail or pincers to pull one out. It gropes about for a signifying intention" (*PM*, 64/45, trans. modified). "The Metaphysical in Man" (1947) emphasized that language is neither an object in front of us nor the product of an internal subjectivity. On the contrary, it must "*surround* each speaking subject" (*SNS*, 107/87); it is almost "in the air" (*P2*, 107). As a result, though there is truly a linguistic milieu in which the speaker "bathes" (in Henri Delacroix's expression adopted by Merleau-Ponty), Merleau-Ponty does not simply transpose the principle he had identified for living things to the sphere of language. On the contrary, the concept of milieu will be redefined in contact with linguistics, moving from the space of an "I can" to a diacritical interval of negation, the "not."

In his description of the "phenomenon of speech and the deliberate act of signification" in *Phenomenology of Perception,* Merleau-Ponty identified the means for leaving behind, "once and for all, the classical subject-object dichotomy" (*PP*, 203/179). In grappling with Saussurean linguistics, he realizes that, since his means are not equal to his ambitions, his treatment of language remains caught in the trap of classic ontology. Saussure, by contrast, in transposing the study of language "into a new milieu" (*RC*, 34/19, trans. modified), is said to have succeeded in conceiving the relationship between speech and signification. He considers speech an articulation between the sign and signification, one that produces a system of intervals that is both differentiation and congruence. Saussure, then, in essence discovered the category of the diacritical, of signs that "function only through their differences, through a certain divergence between themselves and other signs and not, to begin with, by evoking a positive signification" (*SG*, 188/117, trans. modified). Language is neither in the speaker nor in things. Meaning is not hidden in signs; it can emerge, according to Saussure, only from the spacing between them. Signification is not to be sought *in* words or *on* them ("the meaning is not on the phrase like butter on the bread" [*VI*, 201/155, trans. modified]). To be more precise, "to say that no sign signifies by itself, that language always refers back to language because at any moment only a few signs are received, is also to say that language is expressive as much through what is *between* the words as through the words themselves" (*PM*, 62/43). As a result, concludes Merleau-Ponty, language is essentially negative (*PPE*, 81/63), inasmuch as—I would add—it is situated only *between* what it is not and that through which it appears.

To clarify the role of the interval in signification, Merleau-Ponty places the discoveries of the Genevan linguist within the perspective of theories on language acquisition. Although children imitate sounds beginning in the first months of their life, the signifying value of these sounds is not yet understood. Children do not come to understand the link between sound and signification by accumulating particular sounds but rather by intuiting a general coherence. In Roman Jakobson's expression, the phonematic system traces out meaning "as a negative space as it were" (*PPE*, 24/16, trans. modified), and an understanding of that potentiality for signification precedes any particular understanding. The result, again according to Jakobson, is a phenomenon of reduction and "deflation": When a child understands the principle of discrete phonemes, he or she restricts his or her own expressions to fit the needs of communication. In other words, the child must learn to handle his or her powers of spacing.

This phenomenon can be compared to applause at the end of a concert. When the musicians have succeeded in casting a spell over the audience through a performance perceived to be exceptional, the tension that has accumulated over the course of the concert is released, reversing itself into an irrepressible desire on the part of listeners for ecstatic communion by means of applause. After a greater or lesser interval of time, however, the outburst of sound becomes organized, giving way to clapping in unison. It is interesting to note that the common accord does not come about by audience members adjusting to some standard applauder clapping more vigorously than the rest. Rather, they tune in to a general rhythm that gradually breaks through the wave of sound. The most prominent expression thus emerges, oddly enough, not from an amplification but from an interruption: Each audience member has to suspend the beat of one's own clapping to conform to that movement, like the ebb of a wave emerging from the deep, a dynamic that belongs properly to no one but is also outside no one. This is hardly a potentiality in the sense of *ich kann* (Husserl)—perpetuated in the *je peux* of *Phenomenology of Perception*—but rather a potentiality of suspension. Rather than the confirmation of a capacity through its actualization, it is tantamount to a suspension of actualization, a sort of capacity for the *not*.[23]

In short, the matter at hand is no longer to reduce the language/speech pair to the potentiality/act binary but to rethink the virtualities already lodged in any act of speech, even an apparently saturated one. Although linguistics allows Merleau-Ponty to conceive of the virtuality of meaning within speech, he seems to assume that a theory of pure difference—of a mere gap—that would deliberately reject any material determination is condemned to remain abstract. "As pure differences, [the opposing terms] are indiscernible. Expression is a matter of reorganizing the things said, inflecting them with a new curve index, bending them to a certain topography of meaning" (SG, 26–27/19, trans. modified). Indeed, for Merleau-Ponty—and this may be what prevents him from being identified with deconstruction—signs are not simply free-floating. "The elements taken one by one are arbitrary," Merleau-Ponty concedes in an unpublished note (MBN 11, fol. 65), but the relationship among them is not arbitrary.[24] One must abandon the idea that "the relationship between the sign and the signified is a purely external connection, like that between a telephone number and a name, for there is an internal relationship among the signs, taken as an articulate whole, with the signified, taken as field" (ibid.).[25] Although the relationship between sign and signification is no longer a relationship of essence, it does not become purely arbitrary, as a certain interpretation of Saussure would have it.[26] Rather it is organized in terms of processes of agglomeration. The metaphor Merleau-Ponty uses to clarify that centripetal curve is that of an arch (SG, 64/39): The form of an arch, composed of different stones, lies entirely in the arrangement of its elements (without the use of mortar), and these elements assume a meaning and a place within the organized form. As a result, meaning is not born *in* signs but at their fringes or along their edges (SG, 66/40).

Even before Merleau-Ponty used the word "diacritical," he articulated the principle in a lecture titled "The Film and the New Psychology," delivered on March 13, 1945, at the Institut des Hautes Études Cinématographiques (SNS, 61–75/48–59). In this paper he returns to the view held by physiologizing psychology, namely, that our visual field is nothing but a mosaic of sensations, each depending on a local retinal excitation. The new empirical results in psychology would show that, on the contrary, the retina is far from a surface of homogeneous inscription and that, though some of its parts are blind to certain colors (blue or red), there are no holes in our vision. That is because perception always extends beyond the mere act of recording; as it turns out, it is always already a reorganization of the raw sensations. Although there is no organization of or natural cohesion among sensations, we have always already reconfigured them, thus conferring a meaning, albeit incipient, on them. What Walter Benjamin said of the concept—that it is never anything but a *constellation*—would be true a fortiori of perception, which is both "constellated" and "constellating," already formed and at the same time formative. Like the ancients, we arrange the points of the firmament into groups, forming configurations that often have an astonishing longevity (simply consider astronomical constellations, which no one in the West would think to call into question), even though other ways of connecting the dots would be perfectly possible.

When, for example, we are presented with the series {*a b c d e f g h i j*} in the following configuration:

$$a\ b \rightarrow c\ d \rightarrow e\ f \rightarrow g\ h \rightarrow i\ j$$

$$\cdot\ \cdot \rightarrow \cdot\ \cdot \rightarrow \cdot\ \cdot \rightarrow \cdot\ \cdot \rightarrow \cdot\ \cdot$$

we will systematically arrange the points into pairs, as a-b, c-d, e-f, etc., even though, in principle, the pairings b-c, d-e, and f-g would also be possible. To opt for that second pairing, however, would be to invert the distribution of roles between figure and ground. That is what occurs, for example, in the pathological hallucinations of a patient who, contemplating the wallpaper in his or her bedroom, sees something that had previously been only the unperceived ground coming suddenly, obsessively, to the fore. "The idea we have of the world would be overturned if we could succeed in seeing the intervals between things (for example, the space between the trees on the boulevard) as objects and, inversely, if we saw the things themselves—the trees—as the ground" (*SNS*, 62/48–49).

The great aborted project of *Introduction to the Prose of the World* can be summed up as an effort to consider that "object" (the interval of meaning), to bring to light its multiple operations, and to restore to it its value as possibility.

Embodiment and Effacement

The suggestive title of the set of texts posthumously published in 1969 as *The Prose of the World* has its origin in Hegel. As Merleau-Ponty pointed out in a letter to Martial Guéroult in 1951 (*P2*, 45), the trope is to be found in Hegel's considerations of history, in which the Roman state is characterized as the prosaic version of the world. Unlike Hegel's all-embracing scheme, Merleau-Ponty's project did not originally have such a vast ambition—a "sociological signification," Merleau-Ponty would say (ibid.; quoted in *PM*, 13/xiii, trans. modified). As a matter of fact, it was conceived primarily as a sketch on aesthetics[27] in response to Sartre's then-influential *What Is Literature?* Merleau-Ponty, as his reading notes attest, would meticulously study that poetics of *engagé* writing, which Sartre published in *Les Temps Modernes* in 1947. These notes leave no doubt about Merleau-Ponty's assessment: He could not abide that "dialectic of literature," particularly the naïve opposition between prose and poetry. He therefore sets out to write "a sort of *What Is Literature?*" (reading note, quoted in *PM*, 14/xvi) that would deal more specifically with the problem of the sign—the influence of Saussure is apparent—as well as the problem of prose, understood here in its purely literary sense.

Let us recall what Merleau-Ponty wrote in the chapter on speech in *Phenomenology of Perception,* a book Sartre read before composing his essay on literature. Despite the problematic assumptions already indicated, in that chapter Merleau-Ponty formally challenges any subjectivist interpretation of language: Speech is not the translation of an idea; language is, to quote Kurt Goldstein, "no longer a means. Rather, it is a manifestation" (*PP*, 229/202). According to Sartre, who transplants the question to literary soil, one must distinguish clearly between prose and poetry, prose being only a "certain kind of instrument," a means for realizing an aim and hence "in essence utilitarian."[28] By contrast, in Sartre's view poetic speech resists all manipulation and can never be turned into an instrument. In short, says Sartre, the opposition between poetry and prose can be summed up as the distinction between a transparent mode and an opaque one. There is prose when, quoting Valéry's expression, "the word lets our gaze pass through it like the sun through glass."[29] Conversely, there is poetry when words are "inside out,"[30] when the sign presents itself in its opaque objectivity. As a result, Sartre is opposed to the use of a literary style: Whereas the poet must manifest the resistance of signs, the prose writer must conceal his style, make it invisible, since it would divert readers from the content. "Since words are transparent and since the gaze looks through them, it would be absurd to slip frosted glass in among them."[31]

Although Merleau-Ponty almost never designates Sartre by name, his working notes unequivocally indicate that for him *What Is Literature?* plays the role of a negative horizon of sorts. Within the context of preparations for the 1952–53 course on the literary use of language, when Merleau-Ponty once again immersed himself in Valéry's poetry, he again summons forth Sartre, as if to better distinguish himself from him. In an undated working note, he observes, for example: "The poetry of V[aléry] is not, as Sartre says of the surrealists, language turned inside out, words as things, it is not language right side out—words as instruments to deal with things, pincers, antennae (Sartre)—it is sideways language, taken in its lateral unity as a word organism, it is the world [in its] prelogical unity" (MBN 11, fol. 72). There can thus be no contradiction between the transparency of prose and the opacity of poetry; rather, one must seek the common ground between prosaic language and figurative language. Both would *manifest* something that is not in them, without that "*thing to be said* which is before us [being] distinct from any speech" (*PM*, 158/112, trans. modified). Implicitly, Merleau-Ponty reproaches Sartre for treating language as a preformed register that is either in operation or idle. "For the writer, thought does not direct language from the outside" (*P2*, 45); the writer must submit to the inertia of signs, the limits of modulations. But all great prose, in thus "seizing on" the signifying instrument, does nothing but re-create it incessantly within the interval (ibid.). It would therefore be absurd to say that the poet—unlike the prose writer—does not "utilize" language and that these two modes are therefore absolutely "incommunicable."[32] For Merleau-Ponty, every language is utilization of the panoply of expression, all language *gives form* by deforming. That deformation is not arbitrary, however; it is subject to what Malraux called "coherent deformation" and what Merleau-Ponty calls "systematic variation" (*P2*, 44). The "prose" designated by Merleau-Ponty would not stand opposed to poetry or even be restricted to literature; it would become prose *of* and *in* the world, incessantly taking up and "relaunching," like a shuttlecock (Merleau-Ponty borrows the image from Ernst Cassirer), the possibilities of signification and the horizons of meaning.

For Merleau-Ponty, then, it would be preposterous to divide language's transparency and opacity between prose and poetry. Nevertheless, Sartre's reflections seem to turn his idea of transparency in a new direction. Indeed, though Merleau-Ponty used that idea to cast aspersions on the shortcomings of intellectualism and would continue to designate any reductive act of apprehension by that name, transparency, thanks to the study of expression, in some sense becomes more complicated because it is identified as a property of language itself. In *Phenomenology of Perception*, Merleau-Ponty writes that speech "forgets itself as a contingent fact, it relies upon itself and, as we have seen, this gives us the ideal of a thought without speech" (*PP*, 221/196, trans. modified). We have seen how the texts that would come to constitute *Introduction to the Prose of the World* pursued the critique of "a thought without speech." In addition, however, the idea of a "self-forgetting" or "self-oblivion" on the part of language, already thematic in that statement from the 1945 book, would now recur. "The Science and Experience of Expression" begins with the words: "Now, one of the effects of language is to make one forget it to the extent that its expression comes across" (*PM*, 15/10, trans. modified). The notion of language becoming imperceptible, effacing itself before the meaning it conveys (*PM*, 17/10), implies that transparency is not only an ideal of thought but the condition of expression. "In the way it works, language hides itself from us. Its triumph is to efface itself" (*PM*, 16/10). A first hint of that idea can be found in

Phenomenology, when Merleau-Ponty compares language to Proust's description of La Berma in *The Guermantes Way,* where "the actress becomes invisible, and it is Phaedra who appears" (*PP,* 213/188).

Merleau-Ponty insists that this "virtue" of self-effacement on the part of language, to which he will dedicate many pages, goes hand in hand with its embodiment. It is important to note that it is in describing the linguistic phenomenon specifically that Merleau-Ponty manages to dismantle the opposition between the transparency of ideality and the plenitude of the body, articulating them in a new relationship. The medium of meaning (whether gesture, letter, or voice) operates only through a relative self-effacement that we could call, in the very etymological sense of the word, an "an-aesthesia." That an-aesthesia can take place only because there is a sensible foundation to meaning. It is therefore clear why the Husserlian theory of embodiment (*Verleiblichung*)—generally interpreted as the embryo of Merleau-Ponty's phenomenology of the flesh—cannot be conceived without its opposite, namely, self-effacement, the "invisibilization" of the material, sensible signifiers.

In that sense, his consideration of reciprocal dependence goes beyond a certain strain of semiology inherited from Saussure and also beyond Husserl's theory of signs in *Logical Investigations.* There is in fact a striking similarity between the examples in the *Course on General Linguistics* and those chosen by Husserl in his phenomenology of signification. To express his notion of the material indifference of the sign—a fundamental concept for his entire semiology—Saussure uses the example of a game of chess, where the material the pawn is made of, its size, its color, and even to a certain degree its form, are a matter of indifference, so long as its meaning within the game's system, its relations to the other signifiers, remains intelligible: "If I use ivory chessmen instead of wooden ones, the change has no effect on the system, but if I decrease or increase the number of chessmen, this change has a profound effect on the 'grammar' of the game."[33] Saussure concludes that everything that does not influence the grammar of the game must be considered "external" to the sign.[34]

Similarly, Husserl (who was surely unfamiliar with the course compiled by Saussure's students in Geneva), explains: "Chessmen are not part of the chess-game as bits of ivory and wood having such and such shapes and colours. Their phenomenal and physical constitution is quite indifferent, and can be varied at will. They become chessmen, counters in the chess-game, through the game's rules which give them their fixed *games-meaning.*"[35] The historical blindness to a question that is not just hyletic but properly *material* on the part of semiology and a certain strain of phenomenology would thus seem to be explained by the categorial indifference of the material for any theory of signification. Although Merleau-Ponty insists many times on the fundamental contributions of both Saussurean linguistics and Husserl's *Logical Investigations,* he reproaches them for not having considered the corporeal dimension of the sign. The material support (*Zeichenträger*) does not simply represent a negligible quantity or superfluous third term in any relationship between signifier and signified (*Bezeichnendes/Bezichnetes*); rather, as a medium, it makes that relationship possible. This indifference turns out to be not simply the product of an antimaterialist mode of thought (and indifference therefore cannot be turned around into an overt materialism of signification) but rather indicates a *phenomenal* indifference, a nonthematization in appearing itself.

What remains to be considered is no longer simply the relationship between visibility and invisibility, characteristic of the figure/ground structure of Gestalt psychology and the thing/horizon structure of classic phenomenology, but rather the relative imperception already entailed by any embodiment of meaning, which the later Husserl speaks of in *Formal and Transcendental Logic.*[36] Language can never lie beyond signs, beyond its material reactualizations; and yet language is not contained in them, since meaning is not immanent in language (*SG*, 68/42). To conceive of language in terms of its becoming is to criticize all positions that conceive it as an already completed state. Attempts to formalize language fall short in that, despite everything, their generative theory is conceived only in terms of the already performed language act, the *Said*. Formalization, to which the chapter in *The Prose of the World* titled "The Algorithm and the Mystery of Language" is devoted, can set in place a "certain number of transparent relations" only because it relies on what is portrayed as the "adult form of language" (*PM*, 9/5, trans. modified). Likewise, Jean Piaget's theory of language acquisition on the part of children, though presented as a generative theory, ultimately reduces potentiality to action, in that it always describes language learning from the adult perspective (*PPE*, 143/143).

We must place ourselves at the very site of language in the process of making itself—between the given and what makes possible the act of giving—without conceiving of *Saying* on the basis of the already *Said* but also without relegating language to a sphere of pure potentiality, without isolating an abstract linguistic structure or yielding entirely to a completed embodiment in a concrete signifying formula. We must describe at "the juncture of signs" in their "bodily composition" (*PM*, 169/120–21) the bursting forth of that *sense-making*, which is immaterial but just the same not ideal: Rather, the nature of meaning has to be defined as *diacritical.*[37]

From the Literal to the Lateral

Merleau-Ponty, then, seeks to break new ground in his philosophy on the question of the "transparent body of language" (*PM*, 67/48). This philosophy would not confine itself to the reinsertion of meanings into a living body but would make the body itself a "diacritical system" (*N*, 285/222) subtended by latencies, riddled with holes.[38] Although language is not in the body through which it gives itself, it is also not elsewhere. Language is that *dia*, the interstices where phenomena differentiate themselves from one another, a distinction that precedes any act of the "subject," any doing on the subject's part and any dualism. Merleau-Ponty also calls this the "interval . . . in relation to non-difference or in-difference" (*P2*, 272).

In some sense, thought must conform itself to the very movement of that differentiation preliminary to all difference, must coil itself in the dehiscences of signs. And "it is the lateral relation of one sign to another which makes each of them significant, so that meaning appears only at the intersection of and as it were in the interval between words" (*SG*, 68/42). This means that thought will itself have to become lateral, indirect; otherwise, it would risk further substantializing the gap, the interval. Merleau-Ponty does not entirely avoid that temptation when he recommends considering "speech before it is spoken, the background of silence which does not cease to surround it" or even uncovering "the threads of silence that speech is mixed together with" (*SG*, 75/46). How can one not be drawn to that purity of the supporting framework, where one can dream of leaving behind the promiscuous mixing of improper speech? "The philosopher speaks," Merleau-Ponty would later write, "but this is a weakness in him, and an inexplicable weakness: he should keep silent, coincide in silence, and rejoin in Being a philosophy that is there ready-made" (*VI*, 164/125). He corrects himself immediately, however, since, despite everything, that coinciding is illusory. Philosophy is no more ready-made in silence than meaning is to be found—by turning away from words once and for all— in the blanks of the page. Hence that "absurd effort" (ibid.), that inescapable obligation to tell over and over again, to take on and seize again that interstitiality, which—unlike Husserl's claim about the horizon—can never be "possessed."[39]

So the notion of laterality, which Merleau-Ponty discovers in grappling with linguistics, will come to constitute the guiding model for his later philosophy. The act of leading as-yet mute experience—Husserl's "little phrase," which Merleau-Ponty keeps rehashing[40]—to the pure expression of its own meaning may be nothing more than a putting into words (*VI*, 164/125) of that silence, that "fold in the immense fabric of language" (*SG*, 68/42), that hollowness in appearances. If, as Jean Paulhan has shown, one cannot look that hollowness "in the face," then "one can only think of it 'obliquely,' 'mime,' or 'reveal' its mystery" (*PM*, 163/116). One will have to seek a lateral, diagonal speech, an *oratio obliqua,* as medieval rhetoric put it, for that act of articulation prior to utterance, that process of phenomenalization prior to the crystallized phenomenon. To opt for an oblique gaze is to think of meaning at a remove, to conceive of speech *on the basis* of silence, "as deaf people look at those who are speaking" (*SG*, 75/46). That is undoubtedly the meaning to be given to "Indirect Language," an integral part of *The Prose of the World,* which Merleau-Ponty would separate out and publish in a revised version in *Les Temps Modernes* (1952) under the title "Indirect Language and the Voices of Silence." In 1953, at the very moment he had given up ever writing *The Prose of the World,* he transferred his discoveries about the nature of language to the perceptual situation generally: "Just like language, perception is not an encounter with an ob-ject. The object only ever speaks to me laterally, it reaches me not from the front but from the side" (MBN 10, fol. 204v.; *MSME*, 205). How to track this lateral approach of objects in my field of perception? How to be attentive to what goes unnoticed without being invisible? Here again, we find the idea of philosophy as a method to (en-)counter the *ob-vious,* to go against the grain of what is all too smooth. If what is *ob viam* is what makes us go astray, an indirect approach entails taking this experience seriously, making it a starting point for a new method that—to a certain extent—has ethical implications.[41]

In his late period, Merleau-Ponty will find that position at a remove from language, beginning from what cannot be conceived as a language but which is nevertheless not wholly alien to it, in what will become a privileged interlocutor: painting.[42] A "mute art" par excellence, painting is truly the *voice of silence,* as Malraux liked to say. As voice, however, it is precisely not pure silence; rather, it allows the blanks between things to be heard. It does not speak of something different; it speaks of things *differently.* Indeed, a human being, whether a painter or a mere beholder, will never feel at home in painting as he or she may feel at home in language (*PM*, 156/110). The painting process can never be possessed, contrary to what we might believe about the use of words. That is the sense of doubt Merleau-Ponty detects in Cézanne in the 1942 text called, precisely, "Cézanne's Doubt" (*SNS*, 13–33/9–25)—a permanent uncertainty about mastery over the world and its *means* of expression. The painter's canvas becomes the site of an experience of relinquishment, an exposure to an outside where the protective envelope of everyday language disintegrates. It is therefore not surprising that, in contact with these "voices of silence," the philosophy of language, undertaken after *Phenomenology of Perception,* gradually turns into a reflection on the language of philosophy.

At the discussion of the Société Française de Philosophie in November 1946, Émile Bréhier gave one of the harshest criticisms of Merleau-Ponty's writing, one that has continued to echo even in our own time: "I see your ideas as being better expressed in literature and in painting than in philosophy. Your philosophy results in a novel" (*PrP*, 78/30). Merleau-Ponty did not respond directly. It goes without saying, however, that the question of philosophy's means and of philosophy's relation to nonphilosophy took hold as one of the major problems that Merleau-Ponty sought to solve. The solution could consist neither of an exile outside philosophy nor of its dissolution; it had to lie, rather, in an internal radicalization. In that respect, at the 1945 session it was truly Jean Beaufret who anticipated the necessary movement, when he said that the only reproach he had to "make to the author is not that he has gone 'too far,' but rather that he has not been sufficiently radical. The phenomenological descriptions which he uses in fact maintain the vocabulary of idealism" (*PrP*, 103/41–42).

After having turned language into an object of reflection in its own right, Merleau-Ponty became aware that the question of language was much more than a regional question and that it would decide the fate of any practice of reflection. Any inquiry into the philosophy of language presupposes an inquiry into the language of philosophy. Although Merleau-Ponty would make up his mind to abandon the project of *The Prose of the World,* the question of an *other* language and therefore of a modification in descriptive practice, would persist. Like the act of painting, which brings to light an operative meaning, the question at hand was to find "an operative language, that language that can be known only from within, through its exercise" (*VI*, 166/126). Beyond the dream of coinciding in silence on the one hand and, on the other, a reifying discourse that posits its objects of thought in front of itself, as *ob-iectum* (as so many *Gegen-Ständlichkeiten*), "it would be a language of which [the philosopher] would not be the organizer, words he would not assemble, that would combine through him by virtue of a natural intertwining of their meaning, through an underground trafficking in metaphor—where what counts is no longer the manifest meaning of each word and each image, but the lateral relations, the kinships that are implicated in their transfers and their exchanges" (*VI*, 164/125, trans. modified). In a word, if the question of language had allowed Merleau-Ponty to extract his early philosophy from its overdetermination by the living body, the limits of language considered in itself will now lead him to a reconsideration of the question of the body, whose earlier *over*determination, as we shall see, increasingly takes the form of an *under*determination.

3

Ontology of the Visible

Thinking according to the Image

"The problems posed in *Ph.P.* are insoluble," Merleau-Ponty writes in a working note, "because I start there from the 'consciousness'-'object' distinction" (*VI*, 250/200). Were these self-reproaches warranted? Had not *Phenomenology of Perception* attempted, precisely, to get beyond that impasse by demonstrating how consciousness is inserted into a body and objects into a world? Clearly, that solution was no longer convincing to its author, since the body—one's own body—ultimately remained subject to the sphere of consciousness, and the world was still determined in relation to the things it contained. Without giving up the primacy granted to the perceptive, embodied situation, his analysis of language led him to question whether the terms he used for addressing this situation were really adequate. Hence, to argue that the body and the sensible are primary may not be the same thing as to produce a philosophy *of the* body, in that such a philosophy could never extend beyond the purview of a regional ontology and, moreover, would posit the body as an object, thus remaining within an idealistic language, as Jean Beaufret pointed out. If Merleau-Ponty were to bring the body back into philosophy, he would have to abandon the categories inherited from an intellectualist mode of thought[1] and replace "the notions of concept, idea, mind, representation with the notions of *dimensions,* articulation, level, hinges, pivots, configuration" (*VI*, 273/224). As Mikel Dufrenne notes, Merleau-Ponty thereby inaugurated

58

a new philosophical style: philosophizing without philosophemes.[2] Correlatively, that new language, which rejected the crystal clarity of concepts in seeking more transitory or allusive formulations, allowed him to describe what happens around and between things. He would use fleeting concepts, related to what Husserl in his later writings called "fluent meanings" (*fliessende Bedeutungen*) (*PP*, 61/51), somewhat reminiscent of Bergson's "fluid concepts."

An unpublished note for *The Visible and the Invisible* encapsulating the later Merleau-Ponty's self-criticism, indicates that close correlation between practice and philosophical object: "Our corporeality: do not place at the center as I did in *Ph.P.*: in a sense, it is only the world's hinge, its weight is only that of the world. It is but the power of a divergence [*écart*] from the world" (MBN 6, fol. 222v). In following Merleau-Ponty's analyses of language, we have seen his gradual emancipation from the strictures of a gestural theory of expression. There would thus be an autonomy of meaning, a potentiality for ideation that never takes place completely within its materializations—gestures, words, writing—an independence, then, of linguistic structures from their actualizations. Although Merleau-Ponty undeniably integrated the contributions of Saussure, Jakobson, Lévi-Strauss, and the other structuralists into his thinking, there is a rift between Merleau-Ponty's "structure" and that of the structuralist movement.[3] The discovery of the diacritical allowed him to take his distance from any naturalistic interpretation of expression; nevertheless, the structuralist conception of the diacritical, in reducing it to an immaterial mechanism, fell short. It failed to see the indefectible place of the diacritical within the sensible world, which, by its very presence, introduced a gap, a spacing. In a movement that both revealed and moved beyond what he owed to the diacritical, Merleau-Ponty attempted to give voice to the body in its lateral existence. The being of the body, its corporeality, cannot be conflated with bodies; rather, it manifests how they are joined to one another. And if Saussurean linguistics, in considering only these articulations, pure "differences without positive terms" (*PPE*, 81/63), helped Merleau-Ponty avoid the aporias of a constituting consciousness that *posits* its object, it nevertheless overlooked the fact that this interval is not an abstract difference (any more than it is a "hole," as conceived by Hegelianism, even Sartre's version of it)[4] but a sensible juncture, which Merleau-Ponty chose to call a "hinge." A new language—language *in the making*—located between intuitionism and formalism, between positivism and the philosophy of negation, would have to express "at least laterally, an ontogenesis of which it is a part" (*VI*, 137/102).

In the foreword to *Phenomenology of Perception* (1945), the real still formed a "solid fabric" (*PP*, v/lxxiv, trans. modified) on which the entire task of a phenomenology of perception could rest. But Merleau-Ponty had now come to recognize an irreducible infra-corporeal ideality forming the reservoir from which human creativity emerges. He therefore sought a procedure that would allow him to formulate the joint presence of the real and that ideality, without allowing one to be reabsorbed by the other. The third phase of the philosopher's oeuvre, then, stands at an equal distance between a phenomenology of perception and a phenomenology of expression; its aim was to excavate the common ground between the 1945 book and the investigations of language, to reconstitute the fabric, its weft and warp, on which something can be given to me as visible and through which words can give an account of it. Such a project entails, Merleau-Ponty held, returning to the very roots of the visible. And since painting has always already preceded philosophy in that task, thought would have to take its cues from pictorial practices.

In that respect, it is no exaggeration to say that Merleau-Ponty's reflections on painting definitively cast off the outer hull of classic aesthetics. He moves from a philosophy of painting to a philosophy *after* painting (in the sense that a painter who imitates Cézanne's style paints "after" Cézanne) or—more exactly—a philosophy *according to* painting, of which *Eye and Mind* would be the first draft. The article, written in Le Tholonet, in southern France, was the last to be completed during his lifetime. In it Merleau-Ponty develops the idea that the object relation is suspended in the pictorial image, because "I do not look at [a painting] as I do at a thing" (*OE*, 23/164). "It is more accurate to say that I see according to it, or with it, than that I *see it*" (ibid.). Among the manuscripts for this article for the review *Art de France,* which the author revised several times, we find an even more explicit note: "What is a *Bild* [image]? It is obvious here that the *Bild* is not looked at as one looks at an object. One looks according to the *Bild.* . . . And that segregation opens . . . What? Not significations (and even less things, like visible things), but *beings*" (MBN 8.2, fol. 346). Everything seems to indicate, then, that Merleau-Ponty, on the basis of an investigation of the image, came to reformulate his undertaking in the terms of an "ontology of the visible" (*VI*, 182/140). "One must compare perception of *Bild* and perception of the thing, but in taking the thing not from its result (the visual picture in itself) but from its ontogenesis" (MBN 8.2, fol. 346).

What, then, is an ontology of the visible? Far from a naïve phenomenology that would merely enumerate what is visible, Merleau-Ponty's object of inquiry is the very being of the visible: "The visible in the profane sense forgets its premises," he writes (*OE*, 30/167), insofar as the visible is still understood as that which is out there, in front of us. By contrast, modern painting teaches us—and here Merleau-Ponty quotes Klee—that the "painter's vision is not a view upon the *outside*" (*OE*, 69/181).[5] It looks toward "this secret and feverish genesis of things in our body" (*OE*, 30/167). The color conjured up on the canvas is neither the repetition of visible things nor their reduction to an idea of the visible. It comes from an "inward gaze" (*OE*, 24/165, trans. modified). Instead of a *repraesentio* in the Kantian sense, a *Vor-stellung* placed before us, we must decipher that "muffled germination" of appearing amid things, of which painting would be the immediate trace. "The picture's alogical essence," we read in the last drafts, "absolute visible to which things, picture, and even the painter (the painter in the picture) co-belong" (*NC*, 390).

According to Merleau-Ponty, in the history of painting no one incorporated that correlation—which cannot be ripped apart—at a deeper level, no one sought to render more intimately the essence of the visible through the visible itself, than Paul Cézanne. In the ontology of the visible he elaborated at the end of his life, Merleau-Ponty takes Cézanne as his starting point and inverts the asymmetry between method and object. The author of *Eye and Mind* concedes that Cézanne's art is also a "figural philosophy of vision" (*OE*, 32/168, trans. modified). More than that, however, Merleau-Ponty evaluates his own process of thinking in terms of pictorial practices. Instead of comparing the "thought in painting" embraced by this rigorously philosophical painter, he makes up his mind to think "in" or "according to" painting himself. *Thinking as a painter* means submitting to the laws of resistance and experiencing feelings within the limits of the sensible. As Cézanne would say repeatedly: "Everything, especially in art, is theory developed and applied in *contact with nature*."

In 1942—even before finishing *Phenomenology of Perception*[6]—Merleau-Ponty wrote "Cézanne's Doubt," an essay that attests to the dazzling speed with which he had assimilated the painter's poetics. The dense web of quotations is sometimes indistinguishable from the philosopher's own investigations. How, he asks, is one to avoid the alternative (and hence the hierarchy) between the natural world and the human world, the perceptual world and the world of the intelligence? Merleau-Ponty reports the remarks of the Provençal painter in dialogue with Émile Bernard. "But aren't nature and art different?" asks Bernard. Cézanne replies, "I want to make them the same" (*SNS*, 18/13). In these dialogues, "it is clear . . . that Cezanne was always seeking to avoid the ready-made alternatives suggested to him: sensation versus judgment; the painter who sees against the painter who thinks; nature versus composition; primitivism as opposed to tradition" (ibid.). Merleau-Ponty sees Cézanne's art neither as a form of painting that aspires merely to reproduce the immediate givens of sensation nor one that reconstructs a world in accordance with an abstract organization. In his paintings he sees the will to manifest a world in its nascent state, a universe making itself. Cézanne, "rather than apply to his work dichotomies belonging more to schools that perpetuate traditions than to the philosophers or painters who found them," paints "matter as it takes on form, the birth of order through spontaneous organization" (ibid., trans. modified).

Although that general judgment remained in place until *Eye and Mind*, some of Merleau-Ponty's other ideas were modified or even abandoned as he became more familiar with the painter's art. In "Cézanne's Doubt," the laborious exercise of the Husserlian *epoché* (the "bracketing" of all beliefs), which brings to light the pre-objective ground against which an emerging world stands out, has its equivalent (or, in Cézannian terms, its "realization") in Cézanne's method of painting. "We live in the midst of man-made objects, among tools, in houses, streets, cities, and most of the time we see them only through the human actions of which they may be the points of application" (*SNS*, 22/16, trans. modified). Cézanne's painting "suspends" these habits, and the human figures are strange, "as if viewed by a creature of another species" (ibid.). In one picture, "there is no wind in the landscape" (ibid.), "no movement on the Lac d'Annecy; the frozen objects hesitate as at the beginning of the world" (ibid.). The painter seems to be coming back to Husserl's primordial earth (*Erde*), "beneath the constituted order of humanity," which reveals to us "the base of inhuman nature on which the painter has installed himself" (ibid., trans. modified).

"The Thing and the Natural World," a chapter from *Phenomenology of Perception*, quotes the words of the art historian Fritz Novotny to reach the conclusion that these landscapes are "those of a pre-world where there were still no men" (*PP*, 372/337). Here, however, the idea of a preworld is nothing less than a synonym for the "natural world" to which one must return, a world that stands in opposition to the "human world." Just a few years later, during the radio lecture series recorded for Radiodiffusion-Télévision Française in 1948 and published under the title *The World of Perception*, Merleau-Ponty explained, in the section titled "Art and the World of Perception," that, on the contrary, the "purity" of art must be restored (*C*, 53/94), and art, far from imitating the world, is "a world of its own" (*C*, 56/96). That second option, which some have tried to interpret as a thesis about the autonomy of art (a notion generally alien to Merleau-Ponty's phenomenology), doubtless stems instead from a more intense reflection on linguistic signs, which share no perceivable traits with their referent yet do not betray it in any way.[7] Both the idea of art's "world of its own" and that of an inhuman "preworld" revealed by painting remain problematic, however, in that they confirm the subjection of the human world to the natural world or vice versa. Merleau-Ponty, by contrast, believes it imperative to conceive of their simultaneity.

The Styles of the World

How, then, are we to understand what perception and expression have in common, while not resorting to a transcendental a priori? In fact, one path had already been indicated. In *Phenomenology of Perception,* no doubt under the influence of Husserl, Merleau-Ponty compares the unity of the world to the unity of style that can be recognized in a person's behaviors or a city's familiar sites (*PP*, 378/342). Paradoxically, Merleau-Ponty seems to have rediscovered the pertinence of the notion of style on reading André Malraux's *Voices of Silence,* which makes it a key for understanding art, even as the book adheres to a rigorously classic semantics.[8] In Malraux's eyes, style constitutes the artist's signature, his mark, his *stylus.* In a passage from *Voices of Silence,* he says style is nothing other than "the means of re-creating the world according to the values of the man who discovers it" (quoted in *SG*, 83/53). As "a fragile human perspective of the eternal world which draws us along according to a mysterious rhythm into a drift of stars" (*SG*, 83/53), style in Malraux's view reiterates the rift between natural world and human world. It cannot fail to open onto a consideration of modern art— where style is at once the imperative and the unique, undisputed belief—as a ceremony glorifying the individual. If, as a passage from *The Creative Act,* the second volume of Malraux's *Psychology of Art,*[9] has it, style is "the expression of a meaning lent to the world, a call for and not a consequence of a way of seeing" (*SG*, 83/53), then there is every reason to speak of an "annexation of the world by the individual" (ibid., trans. modified).

According to Merleau-Ponty, however, style is not produced by a subjectivity: It is a feature of the world as it manifests itself. Far from being confined to the realm of art, style is what in-forms the world; it is the guarantee that a world is never given once and for all but is constantly modulated, articulated, rhythmicized. "Perception already stylizes," Merleau-Ponty claims in a famous passage from *The Prose of the World* (*PM*, 83/59), thereby obliterating the dichotomy between receptivity and activity. It is the correlation itself that undergoes a certain inflection, and that correlation does not precede the dichotomy between receptivity and activity but constitutes its nexus. Husserl may have already glimpsed as much in the manuscripts of *Ideen II* (*PM*, 79/56), where the notion of style is not limited to the permanent, unitary style (*einen gewissen durchgängigen einheitlichen Stil*) of a personality in its judgments and acts. There is also what could be called *habitus* or *overall style* (*Gesamtstil*), a concordant unity that characterizes all the activities (and passivities) of a subject.[10] In *The Crisis of European Sciences,* Husserl will go even further. Style is now characteristic not of an ego but of the world itself: "Thus our empirically intuited surrounding world has an *empirical over-all style* [*empirischen Gesamtstil*]."[11] For the later Husserl, it is in the world that one must seek "that which gives the character of *belonging together* to bodies which *exist together* simultaneously and successively, i.e., . . . that which *binds* their being [*Sein*] to their being-such [*Sosein*]."[12] It would seem that Merleau-Ponty in turn superimposes Husserl's insight onto the successive developments of Heidegger—whom he read carefully in the 1950s—regarding a "style of the *welten* [worlding]." What, in Heidegger's German, could mean either world-being or world-making now indisputably takes on the second sense. To avoid putting style on the side of a "*universal causal regulation*" of the world independent of our variations,[13] Merleau-Ponty understands it as the attribute of a correlation by means of which a world becomes visible; style casts into relief its manner of *welten,* of "world-making." As a result, painting would be nothing but the attempt to manifest that very manifestation, which is prior to the division between human and world. "The painter knows nothing of the antithesis of man and the world . . . since man and signification are sketching themselves against the background of the world through the very operation of style" (*PM*, 83/59).

In that mode of thinking *according to the image,* style will constitute a first stopping point in the descent to the process of appearing. Merleau-Ponty strove tirelessly to return to the near side of the separation between activity and giving and to grasp the enigma of visibility (*OE*, 26/166). Indeed, there is truly a "gift of visibility" in both senses: the fact that something appears to us unexpectedly, although we never asked for it, and the fact that some have the talent to visualize this very event, in the sense that one says of an artist that he is "gifted." Painters are the privileged beneficiaries of that gift; they have the gift of visibility "as it is said that the inspired man has the gift of tongues" (*OE*, 25/165, trans. modified). Through painting, then, Merleau-Ponty will arrive at an ontology of the visible, whose starting point is not visible-as-being-visible but visible-as-becoming-visible. All his later meditations echo a line from Cézanne that will serve as the epigraph for *Eye and Mind*: "What I am trying to translate to you is more mysterious; it is entwined in the very roots of being, in the impalpable source of sensations" (*OE*, 8/159). In willing himself to think like a painter, Merleau-Ponty endeavored to "restore painting and the arts in general to their rightful place . . . [and] allow them to recover their dignity" (*C*, 55/94), even while irremediably broaching the possibility of an autonomy of art of some sort. Art is not an alternative to the natural world but an intensification of its operations. Merleau-Ponty's aesthetics in its entirety is therefore a making-sensible of thought, leading to *dés-oeuvrement,* the putting out of work of the work.[14] Art is no longer to be sought in works but rather in an amplification of the sensible bonds that connect us to the world. These bonds will henceforth be called "flesh."

To compensate for the shortcomings of *Phenomenology of Perception,* Merleau-Ponty does not simply replace "consciousness" and "thing" with "body" and "world," which would risk once again perpetuating ontological dichotomies. Rather, he says, we must install ourselves in the "inter-world," in the "invagination" (*VI,* 197/152) of a "a raw, original being," which, while still the movement of an originary differentiation, precedes any individuation. In his famous analysis in *The Visible and the Invisible,* this diacritical differentiality will be applied to a patch of red color. Merleau-Ponty, invoking the whole range of possible reds, from that of the flags of gatekeepers and of the Revolution, to that of tiled rooftops and the colorful dresses of gypsy women on the Champs-Élysées, to the reddish soil of Madagascar, affirms that red is nothing in itself. Red is not a "chunk of absolutely hard, indivisible being, offered completely naked to a vision that could be only total or nil; it is rather a strait of sorts, always wide-open, between external horizons and internal horizons, something that touches lightly and makes various regions of the colored or visible world resonate at a distance, a certain differentiation, an ephemeral modulation of this world—less a color or a thing, therefore, than a difference between things and colors" (*VI,* 173/132, trans. modified). How to conceive of this difference between things and colors, between objects and qualities, without referring to a transcendental subjectivity that would provide their unity? Merleau-Ponty's approach is to search for a constitutive principle that, rather than being a priori, is materially immanent in the sensible itself. This sensible element (which is to be thought of less as an elemental *atom* than as an elemental fabric) is to be sought in the interstices of perception: "Between the so-called colors and visibilities, we might find anew the fabric that lines them, sustains them, nourishes them, and which for its part is not a thing, but a possibility, a latency, and a *flesh* of things" (*VI,* 173/132–33, trans. modified).

As is clear from the context, Merleau-Ponty's "flesh" is not to be seen as some kind of deeper, more fundamental body. If, as "Indirect Language and the Voices of Silence" already declared, "the meaning of philosophy is the meaning of a genesis" (*SG,* 103/82), then philosophy must abandon the idea that the body—or whatever comes to replace it—represents the promise of access to the origin. On the contrary, philosophy must give up the quest for ultimate positivities and become a genetic phenomenology, radical in the etymological sense of the word: It must dig down deep to the origin, which proves to be, as it were, always already fissured, in order to "accompany this break-up, this non-coincidence, this differentiation" (*VI*, 163/124).

Phenomenology, then, cannot confine itself to a philosophy of genesis. It will have to become a phenomenology of the genesis of genesis—in other words, ontogenetic. Merleau-Ponty's attempt to rethink phenomenology as a whole culminates in a confrontation with an ontological mode of questioning; as a result, phenomenology and ontology, traditionally placed in opposition to each other, come to coincide. The "new ontology" he sought to elaborate in the late 1950s[15] is the exact opposite of a Porphyrian Tree of categories culminating in substantial being. It is rather an "ontological rehabilitation of the sensible" (*SG*, 210/167), a phenomenology of "Being . . . of the depths," one that digs an "abyss" that is unfathomable because bottomless (*VI*, 236/77, trans. modified). The need for a return to ontology that brings to light a "wild," "vertical" Being also reveals the kinship between "the being of the earth and that of my body (*Leib*)" (*RC*, 169/190). The problematic of the milieu as it appeared in the early works is thus radicalized. The body is no longer a "means" in a world-milieu; rather, body and world proceed from a common fabric, belong to a "formative milieu" (*VI*, 191/147, trans. modified).

Ontology of the Flesh

How to name what lies between beings, what sustains them and forms a common thread between them? Merleau-Ponty concedes that this thing "has no name in any philosophy" (*VI*, 181/147) and thus remains literally *anonymous*. Aristotle used the term *anonymos* to indicate that natural language cannot account in equal measure for all the givens of reality. As Aristotle explains, the set of animals equipped with feathered wings was given the name "bird," but language (Greek in this case) remains silent about those animals with membranous or skin wings.[16] The language of scientists, but also that of philosophers, confers names on what had remained empty slots, subsequently revealed through the study of the real (let's remember that in nineteenth-century chemistry, Mendeleev's periodic table anticipated empty slots for certain elements long before these were actually observed). From the late 1940s on, the thing that "has no name in any philosophy," Merleau-Ponty's *anonymos,* having already come to the fore at the end of *Phenomenology of Perception,* will receive an (ambiguous) name, which will come to occupy the center of his later writings: *flesh*. The term is ambiguous in the "bad" sense of the word, both because of its connotations, which have given rise to many misunderstandings,[17] and, no doubt, because it is inadequate for truly naming what is at issue for Merleau-Ponty.

How did these misunderstandings come about? A deep-rooted prejudice would have it that what Merleau-Ponty calls *chair* (and which is commonly translated into English as *flesh*) would be the exact equivalent of Husserl's notion of *Leib*. When Husserl was translated into French, a second term had to be found to capture the terminological distinction that German allows between *Körper* (the physical, objective body) and *Leib* (the lived, experiential body). *Körper* (body-object) was translated as *corps,* and *Leib*, generally, as *chair.* It must have seemed obvious to early commentators of Merleau-Ponty that his use of the notion had to be understood within that context. Hence Theodore Geraets was led to say that Merleau-Ponty's notion of "*la chair* . . . translates exactly what Husserl calls *Leib*."[18] Nothing could be more misleading, however. Despite how often such a statement has been repeated, it stands in open contradiction to Merleau-Ponty's claim that *la chair* "has no name in any philosophy." As Emmanuel de Saint-Aubert has shown, Merleau-Ponty never bothered to distinguish his notion of *chair* from Husserl's notion of *Leib* for the simple reason that he never thought the two would be conflated. Although he provides various translations for *Leib (corps vivant, corps propre)*, Merleau-Ponty does not once use the term *chair* in that context.[19] What is the relevance of such philological questions? They undercut the still-persistent idea that Merleau-Ponty's notion of flesh was, if not an exact equivalent of Husserl's *Leib*, then at least a generalization of it. Merleau-Ponty himself is not totally innocent in this matter: In his "Nature" course, he says that the "flesh of the body makes us understand the flesh of the world" (*N*, 280/218). Is flesh, then, simply a bodily structure that has been generalized to the world as such?

Although some statements may be interpreted to point in that direction, the majority of relevant passages seems to exclude such a reading. Merleau-Ponty expressly refrains from understanding the word "flesh" in terms of a hylozoism of the Leibnizian strain, in which the characteristics of the living thing would simply be transposed onto the nonliving (*VI*, 304/242). A May 1960 note is unambiguous: "The flesh of the world is not explained by the flesh of the body" (*VI*, 298/250). Or, even more plainly: "The 'flesh of the world' is not [a] metaphor of our worldly body. One could put this the other way round: it's rather our body that is made of the same sensible stuff than the world is made of" (*NC*, 211).

These few passages are certainly not sufficient to provide a solution to a long-standing debate within Merleau-Ponty scholarship, and Merleau-Ponty's own exploratory style in the later working notes attests that he was himself ambivalent about the ultimate status of "flesh." Given its reception, one may wonder whether the term itself was not ill-fated from the outset, since it suggests a kind of interiority, whereas Merleau-Ponty was actually looking for the opposite. At one point in the "Nature" course, Merleau-Ponty even offers an alternative—and possibly more felicitous—word for "flesh": *the sensible.* "The sensible is the flesh of the world, that is, sense on the outside" (*N*, 280/218, trans. modified). Sense would therefore be nowhere to be found on the inside, neither in subjects nor in objects, but would emerge in the interstices of their relationship.

Why did Merleau-Ponty not simply use the expression "the sensible"? One can only speculate. A likely explanation is that he feared that such a notion would still be caught up in the subject-object opposition of the metaphysical tradition he was overtly attempting to overthrow. Whereas the notion of the sensible (that which is capable of sensibility) has the advantage of allowing for both an objective and a subjective meaning (that which is capable of being sensed and of being sentient), it is still trapped within a mode of thinking (in terms of alternatives) that Merleau-Ponty's later writings sought to overcome. "Flesh" might have appeared to offer a divergent path: Flesh is neither a sentient being nor an object sensed in itself, but that *through which* something sensible is sensed, its operative medium. As such, the "stuff" that allows for sensibility is specific neither to a single living being nor to a single act of sensing but must belong to the structure of the world. The world is a space where beings can appear insofar as the world is sensible, and it is sensible insofar as it does not itself appear but lets other beings appear, by simultaneously withdrawing and resisting phenomenalization. In a way, it could be argued that "flesh" is Merleau-Ponty's ontophenomenological reformulation of Saussure's notion of the diacritical: *Flesh as embodied diacritical,* as that which structures, introduces spacing, and hence enables the emergence of sense-objects. Flesh would thus be the tentative name to designate this *anonymos,* neither substance nor matter nor spirit, which would therefore be closer to an "element" in the pre-Socratic sense, a generative material that would have no proper place and would nevertheless be everywhere. More than a milieu, but not to be confused with the *Welt,* flesh is both an "ultimate notion" and the fabric underlying Being, "lateral investment" (*VI*, 266/217). Because all flesh is development and envelopment of another flesh, what is prefigured here is the sensible coiled around itself, which offers Merleau-Ponty the model for reflexivity as a whole.

The example chosen to clarify that pre-objective reflexivity returns to the Husserlian problematic of the left hand touching the right.[20] Jacques Derrida, while pointing out in *Voice and Phenomenon* that auto-affection is in some sense the primal scene of phenomenology,[21] overlooks the fact that the reciprocity of touching/touched is not simply the last stage in an ideology of presence; on the contrary, it is the inception of a philosophy of nonpresence and nontransparency. Merleau-Ponty, who is almost systematically left out of Derrida's writings,[22] already affirms that essential paradigm shift in *Phenomenology of Perception*: "When I touch my right hand with my left hand, the object 'right hand' also has this strange property, itself, of sensing." But he adds, precisely, "the two hands are never simultaneously both touched and touching. So when I press my two hands together, it is not a question of two sensations that I could feel together, as when we perceive two objects juxtaposed, but rather of an ambiguous organization" (*PP*, 109/95). And he goes on to say that the meaning of the "double sensations" noted by Husserl is that "in the passage from one function to the other, I can recognize the touched hand as the same hand that is about to be touching; in this package of bones and muscles that is my right hand for my left hand, I glimpse momentarily the shell or the incarnation of this other right hand, agile and living, that I send out toward objects in order to explore them" (ibid.). Insofar as the body surprises itself from the outside in exercising a knowledge function, it "begins 'a sort of reflection'" (ibid.). In so-called reflexive philosophies (also known as German Idealism), the identity between the reflecting and the reflected ensures a perfect epistemic transparency. Here, however, the noncoincidence between the touching and the touched entails an incessant turning back on oneself that cannot be resolved into a permanent state. Beyond any comforting specularity, the reversibility of touching/touched calls for a reflection that is never entirely in possession of itself, a reflection that, more than a reflexive philosophy—which in Hegel "returns to itself" (*SG*, 112/73)—is a twisting, a reversal.

In the edited part of *The Visible and the Invisible*, Merleau-Ponty develops the idea of a "hyper-reflection" to take into account that reversibility, always imminent and never realized (such is the meaning of the statement that reversibility is an "ultimate truth" [*VI*, 201/155]). In opposition to reflexive philosophy, which in its impregnable ivory tower no longer experiences any obstacles, hyper-reflection would exhibit the organic connection from which it arose (*VI*, 60/38) and would in that way remain bound to the self "not through transparence" but "through confusion" (*OE*, 19/162–63). Already *Phenomenology of Perception* "radicalized" reflection, in the sense of going back to the roots, the origins. "Reflection grasps its own full meaning only if it mentions the unreflected ground that it presupposes" (*PP*, 280/289, trans. modified). But what exactly does "the unreflected ground" mean here? Is it not another formulation of what transcendental philosophies understand as a reflection on the "conditions of possibility"? The passages from *Phenomenology of Perception* (which, it must be said, are not very clear) might suggest so. It is not until the chapter "Reflection and Interrogation" in *The Visible and the Invisible* that the irreducibility of the unreflected to reflection will be postulated. If we understand the unreflected as something that reflection has not *yet* thought, says Merleau-Ponty, we overlook its radicality in two respects. First, in considering it as thinkable in the future, we immediately normalize the unreflected, align it with the other objects of reflection; and second, any transcendental philosophy of reflection, in its desire to move beyond experience, overlooks not just a certain radicality but radicality as such. The starting point ought to be not the suspension of perception but faith in it. In place of a philosophy of reflection whose radicality "uproots" thought (*VI*, 66/43), we must dig down to the roots of the embodied being, practice what from here on in will bear the name *hyper-reflection*. Indeed, if I reflect, it is by virtue of my body, which shares the horizon with others, by virtue of a persistent bond that unites me with the world and is not reducible to a simple discursive operation. To reflect on reflection, then, consists less of adding on another degree of abstraction; on the contrary, hyper-reflection must "plunge into the world instead of looking at it from above, it must descend toward it such as it is instead of working its way back up toward a prior possibility of thinking it" (*VI*, 60/38–39, trans. modified). It is not that I place myself back "at the origin of a spectacle that I could never have had unless, unbeknown to myself, I organized it" (*VI*, 67/44); rather, the starting point for the reflection is dislocated onto the experience of the "adversity of the things" (ibid.). Indeed, *there is* truly "some" world, and every time something appears to us, inasmuch as it appears, something *is*. Therefore, to ontologize reflection means nothing other than to reflect on the being from which reflection proceeds, a being that *is for me* and, in equal measure, *of which I am*. A "promiscuous Being," an "enveloping being" (*SG*, 30/22, trans. modified), a being in which I am inherent but also, without my ever renouncing it, a being that appears to me, a being phenomenalizing itself and giving itself on the outside, an outside that is always receding.

To conceptualize that duality, Merleau-Ponty makes use of the rhetorical figure of the chiasm. Like the letter χ (chi) of the Greek alphabet from which its name is derived, a chiasm is composed of nonparallel lines, each of which binds two elements together. These lines intersect in the middle,

Figure 1

an indication of the interdependence of the linked terms. In the most simple scenario, a chiasm articulates a relationship of inversion among four terms, each placed at one corner of a square (see Figure 1).

But this diagram overlooks the fact that the chiasm, in its poetic and rhetorical usage, is never visible but unfolds as one reads a text or listens to spoken language. In Baudelaire's short but extraordinary poem "À une passante" ("To a Woman Passing By," 1855), we find a chiasm that could almost go unnoticed:

Car j'ignore où tu fuis, tu ne sais où je vais
For I know not where you flee, you don't know where I go

In the first place, this is a grammatical chiasm, the most common kind: The pair of personal pronouns, I/you, in the first part of the line is inverted in the second, becoming you/I. A semantic chiasm complements the grammatical one (know not / don't know—flee / go), which, in its very repetition, underscores the change that has occurred. In the following line, Baudelaire confirms the complicity born in the furtive moment of that fortuitous encounter:

Ô toi que j'eusse aimée, à toi qui le savais!
O you whom I might have loved, to you who knew it!

The intertwining of the two people at the point where they briefly cross paths remains, but it has become increasingly virtual, because the two movements (go / flee) are centrifugal and divergent. The verbs Baudelaire uses in the previous line take on a new meaning, and the spatial dimension is transformed into a moment in time. "For I know not where you flee, you don't know where I go": if we read "où tu *fuis*" as having the effect of a paronym of "où tu *fus*" ("where you were," *fus* being the *passé simple* of *être*, to be), then an entire existential dimension unfolds. In other words, *fuis/ fus* points to the impenetrable history of the anonymous passerby *before* the encounter, whereas "where I go" indicates the speaker's future and inscrutable horizons.

The example from Baudelaire demonstrates the principal characteristics of the rhetorical chiasm, which Merleau-Ponty retains in his notion of ontological chiasm. The close relationship between the terms indicates a simultaneous co-implication ("the idea of *chiasm*, that is: every relation with being is *simultaneously* a taking and a being taken" [*VI*, 313/266]). And yet the chiasm cannot be carried over to a structural schema in which the terms could be inverted at will. If such were the case, Merleau-Ponty's notion of chiasm would indeed simply be, as Levinas asserted, another figure for the metaphysical concept of reversibility, in which "the terms are *indifferently* read from left to right and right to left."[23] That allegation of symmetricality remains to be proven, however, since it leaves out some of the most crucial aspects of the chiasmatic relationship.

As a matter of fact, the key lies once again in the fact that the structure Merleau-Ponty describes is not abstract but fundamentally situated. In other words, the chiasm is of a perspectival nature, and, as a result, it can always only be considered—as attested by its deployment over time—with reference to one of the terms in the relationship. Along with a simultaneity of co-belonging, then, there is a real asymmetry in any relationship of the type $a \rightarrow B / B \rightarrow a$ (and Levinas has identified the ethical stakes of such an asymmetry). This asymmetry is literally complicated, in that the chiasm does not allow one to determine definitively a "high" and a "low" position. In the chiasmatic relationship, the asymmetry is replicated, duplicated, in the form of a cross ($a \rightarrow B / B \rightarrow a \mid A \rightarrow b / b \rightarrow A$), thus guaranteeing a divergence within inherence, a noncoincidence within simultaneity.

The elaboration of the idea of chiasm may therefore constitute one of the best ways to escape the *clinamen* of transparency, which inevitably leads thinking to become conflated with its objects. Phenomenology, in proceeding according to the image of a chiasm, holds onto the idea of an originary intertwining but offers more resistance to the inevitable temptation of reductionism. To permanently undo the knot of the relationship, to bring it back to a crystalline relation, is to lose it forever. Instead of cutting the Gordian knot, the new ontology of the chiasm opts to plunge deeper into the knottedness of sensible experience, where a co-belonging in noncoincidence takes shape. That cohesion is not produced by a conceptual reconstruction *post factum*; rather, it is a cohesion of conceptless adherence.

Even so, it does not give up the ideality of reflection—the precondition for taking one's distance from the given—since to locate it in the supra-sensible would be to miss the point: "There is a strict ideality in experiences that are experiences of the flesh: the moments of the sonata, the fragments of the light field, adhere to one another with a conceptless cohesion" (*VI*, 196/152, trans. modified). In that way, the new ontology—an ontology of proximal adherence—will not only analyze the sensible as a privileged object; it will find in the sensible the model for its own armature. We move from an ontological reestablishment founded on the sensible toward an aesthesic description of the beams and joists of Being.

Touching the Visible

"To touch and to touch oneself (to touch oneself = touched-touching) They do not coincide in the body," notes Merleau-Ponty in May 1960. But he adds: "This does not mean that they coincide 'in the mind' or at the level of 'consciousness.' Something else than the body is needed for the junction to be made" (*VI*, 302/254). At this point, Merleau-Ponty introduces a surprising notion: The other-than-the-body where the junction is made is "the untouchable" (ibid.). This is a troubling category at first sight, so freighted is it with assumptions both metaphysical and religious. Merleau-Ponty hastens to explain that this is not a negation (normative or logical) of touching: "The untouchable is not a touchable that is de facto inaccessible" (ibid., trans. modified).[24] Beyond a symmetry between touching and touched, which, through mutual envelopment, guarantees the reversibility of the two terms, there is truly something in the tangible that resists total inversion, and which Merleau-Ponty calls "untouchable" (*l'intouchable*). It is as if touching contained a dimension of imperception, an irreducible *punctum caecum,* a blind spot signaling toward the back side of sensible Being (*VI*, 303/255). It is striking that, in Merleau-Ponty's writings, the question of touch invariably spills over into a metaphorics—even a problematics—of vision, and that, conversely, the problematics of the visible is continually brought back to a semantic register of touching.[25]

What is the meaning of that chiasm between the tangible and the visible? And are the two orders really commensurable? Jacques Derrida aptly points out that, in this same note of May 1960, Merleau-Ponty opened a parenthesis on the invisible when addressing the question of the untouchable. "The untouchable (and also the invisible: for the same analysis can be repeated for vision . . ." But the parenthesis on the invisible is never closed, and the return to the untouchable will never take place.[26] The question remains open: Why, among the many titles considered for his second magnum opus, did Merleau-Ponty never opt for *The Touchable and the Untouchable*? Why will what was presented as a parenthesis interior to the question of the body's tactility shatter that frame, establishing the realm of an ontology of the "visible and the invisible"? Is it true, as Claude Lefort asserted, that Merleau-Ponty's entire oeuvre converges on the question "What Is Seeing?"[27] Reflections such as "To be sure, our world is principally and essentially visual; one would not make a world out of scents or sounds" (*VI*, 113–14/83) seem to leave no room for ambiguity. Might Derrida be right, then, when—against the view that Merleau-Ponty rehabilitated the sense of touch—he accuses him of being one of the last representatives of "photological metaphysics," which, since Heraclitus[28] or Aristotle,[29] has privileged vision over all the other senses? Is Merleau-Ponty yet another agent of the alleged "denigration of touch" in Western philosophy?[30]

To answer that question, we must consider the relation between vision and touch in "The Philosopher and His Shadow" and the implicit redefinition of that relation in Merleau-Ponty's reading of Husserl's *Ideen II*. In this article, Merleau-Ponty is primarily concerned with §§36 and 37 in Husserl's manuscripts (which were not published until 1952, but which Merleau-Ponty had consulted at Leuven), in which the philosopher shows how, at the level of *Leiblichkeit*, the distinction between subject and object is seemingly blurred by the fact that the living body is *double*, both a physical thing and a source of sensations. When the right hand touches the left, the left hand ceases to be a mere physical object (*bloss physisches Ding*); it "becomes body" (*es wird Leib*).[31] In moving beyond the dualism between "constituting consciousness" and "constituted world," the later Husserl thus undeniably grants to touch a privilege he denies to vision. In fact, there is in the primal experience (*Urerlebnis*) of the touching-touched hand an experience of constituting one's own body that is not so much dualist as bifid, an experience Husserl will then extend to bodies other than one's own (*Fremdkörper*) and to nature. By means of that perception, he will go so far as to write, in *Cartesian Meditations*, "I experience . . . my own body, which therefore in the process is reflexively related to itself."[32] Not only does it seem that this antepredicative reflection could "play out beyond the visual sphere"; Husserl will even come to deny the reflexivity of the gaze. According to him, if one were to hypothesize a purely ocular subject, he would have no phenomenal body, since his own body would appear to him as a purely material thing.[33] From the outset, then, the gaze separates the local sphere of one's own feeling body from the sphere of the perceived sensible objects. The example of perceiving oneself in a mirror cannot be invoked either, since it is only after the fact that one reconstitutes the seeing eye, indirectly and by means of "empathy" (*Einfühlung*). As a result, vision will never attain the reversibility of touching and touched; I can never perceive the seeing eye as seeing (*das sehende Auge als sehendes*).[34] I can touch my hand touching, whereas the eye that appears to me in the mirror is not presented as seeing but rather as one visual element among others. For Husserl, then, there is expressly a privilege (*Vorzug*) of touch over the other senses—even over the sense that, since Aristotle, has been called "the most noble."[35] In §37, which is devoted to the "differences between the visual and tactual realms," he endeavors to challenge the transposition of tactile qualities onto looking: "To be sure, sometimes it is said that the eye is, as it were, in touch with the Object by casting its glance over it. But we immediately sense the difference."[36]

If, therefore, it is possible to speak of a "collapse of any parallelism between vision and touch" that Husserl had established,[37] how are we to explain that Merleau-Ponty restores that parallelism without explanation and even justifies it by citing the example of Husserl? Indeed, though Merleau-Ponty observes in a note that vision and touch are "not superposable" and that "one of the universes overhangs the other" (*VI*, 304/256), it is indisputable that he not only reestablishes the parallelism—"we could not possibly touch or see without being capable of touching or seeing ourselves" (*S*, 23–24/16)—but also goes so far as to reverse the priorities, replacing the "surprising ontological privilege" that Husserl granted to touch with an "exorbitant privilege" of sight.[38] Nevertheless, we must still come to an understanding of what that reversal means, since the privilege given to sight does not necessarily entail a return to an "oculocentrism" of the metaphysics of presence. When Merleau-Ponty makes flesh a "visible thing par excellence," he defines the sensible as both *inherence* and *distance* (and the fate of phenomenology hangs in the balance of every nuance). Recall that the experience of touching/touched had allowed Husserl to move beyond the dualism between subjective sensation and objective perception, as it existed in the epistemology of Hermann von Helmholtz and the dominant conception of physiology in the late nineteenth century, toward a characterization of one's own body (*Eigenleib*) no longer as constituted but as self-constituting. Even so, Husserl realizes that, though such an approach can account for immediate "archipresence" (*Urpräsenz*), it is incapable of describing the giving in "co-presence" or even "absence." As he will note in §42, that approach "from the inside" remains trapped in a solipsistic position. Parallel to that phenomenology of *Urpräsenz*, Husserl will develop, on the model of vision, a phenomenology of "appresentation" (*Appräsenz*), where the sensation in one's own body is achieved only a posteriori, by empathy or feeling-into (*Einfühlung*).

The later Merleau-Ponty takes on precisely that aporia between solipsism and naturalism, which Husserl does not believe can be resolved through a juxtaposition of the two. Noncoincidence is not to be sought in separation or absence: It lies at the very heart of the experience of feeling/felt. In opposition to a philosophy of pure archipresence as it emerges in Husserl's description of the touching/touched body, Merleau-Ponty confers on that body the characteristic of vision, that is, the constitutive gap between seeing and seen: "Vision is not a certain mode of thought or presence to self; it is the means given me for being absent from myself, for being present at the fission of Being" (*OE*, 81/186). In determining flesh as visibility par excellence, he does not return to a heliotropic philosophy of immediate intuition, but takes the exact opposite path. What he outlines rather is an ontology of absence in presence, inherence in distance.

For Merleau-Ponty, this entails redefining the meaning of touch and vision and their relation, and he does not limit that redefinition to declarations of intentions and programmatic announcements that paradigms have shifted. Rather, he excavates these paradigms from the inside and proceeds, therefore, to an immobile overtake, a "surpassing in place" (*VI*, 198/153, trans. modified). That return to *within* the Western philosophical tradition (with analyses of Descartes and Hegel in particular, to whom Merleau-Ponty's last courses at the Collège de France were devoted) then takes on the features of a Heideggerian "Erinnerung *in* die Metaphysik," a remembrance *into* metaphysics, as a means to bring to light unthought presuppositions.

Diplopia

In the plan dating to January 1959 and still bearing the title of the work announced in 1952, "The Origin of Truth,"[39] Merleau-Ponty announces a "reflection on Descartes's ontologies—the 'strabism' of Western ontology" (*VI*, 217/166).[40] We can only conjecture about the meaning of the dash (does it unite or separate, mark an identity or a juxtaposition?), but we cannot dismiss the plural form Merleau-Ponty gives to Cartesian ontology. Could the diversity and contradictions of Descartes's ontological positions shed light on the ambiguity that seems to characterize Western ontology? Before answering that question, it is necessary to emphasize that the later Merleau-Ponty did not suddenly discover that he was a historian of philosophy. As he explains in the last course he taught in 1960–61, "Cartesian Ontology and Present-Day Ontology," he was hardly seeking to restore "what Descartes said, in the order in which he said it, in answer to his problems," as Martial Guéroult understood it,[41] or to impose "our problems" on him (*NC*, 223). There is no philosopher within the tradition to whom

Merleau-Ponty returned more persistently than Descartes, from the early chapters of *Phenomenology of Perception* to the book that lay open on his work table at the moment of his death, the treatise *Optics*.[42] This can perhaps be explained by the resistance provided him by Cartesian thought, attributable both to the extreme proximity of the questions he and Descartes were asking and to the supreme distance in how they treated them. It is striking that the question of vision runs through Merleau-Ponty's interpretation of Descartes like a guiding thread. Whether within an epistemological context, such as the chapter on the cogito in *Phenomenology of Perception,* or in his reflections on the sciences in *Eye and Mind,* or finally, within an ontological context, in the class notes and the notes for *The Visible and the Invisible,* Merleau-Ponty seems to associate Descartes's name with a certain *vision* of things, a vision pursued far beyond the historical figure to the very bedrock of the Western tradition. What, then, does that "strabism," that double vision, consist of?

It is noteworthy that, from *The Structure of Behavior* on, Merleau-Ponty's writings oppose dualisms, which will take the form, by turns, of intellectualism and empiricism, intuitionism and naturalism, *criticisme* (critical philosophy) and positivism. To privilege one term over another would once again be to move along the ground of a "bad dialectics" (to use Hegel's vocabulary), in which, since no position can contain its opposite, the dialectic remains unstable in the sense chemists give that word, constantly decomposing and recomposing, which would make any *position,* precisely, impossible. Even Hegel's synthetic dialectic does not escape that movement, since it still presupposes a single viewpoint, from which the synthesis could be carried out "from above." To escape that unstable position, Merleau-Ponty practices from the start what he will later call a "hyperdialectic"— and which, in contrast to Hegel's method, might rather be called an *infra-* or *hypo*dialectic—which commentators early on termed a "philosophy of ambiguity."[43] Yet the last texts indicate that Merleau-Ponty was seeking to give a different foundation, both historico-philosophical and ontological, to that ambiguity, which, subsequent to an analysis of vision in Descartes, would take the name "visual dualism," or "diplopia." Merleau-Ponty finds in Descartes the exordium of dualist metaphysics, and, far from rejecting it outright, he will excavate that metaphysics to bring to light the causes of dualism.[44]

Descartes saw vision in the material sense (vision in the flesh) as scandalous because it was "action at a distance." Therein lay both its difficulty and its virtue (*OE,* 37/169). Various texts, from the *Optics* to *Rules* and *Meditations,* would thus express the need to stabilize that hybrid vision by polarizing it, to better exorcise the specters it produces (*OE,* 36/169). The "enigma of vision," this thing that is neither here nor elsewhere but properly "ubiquitous," would thus be wrenched apart and assigned two different locations, one in the physical realm and one in the mind. Thanks to the emergence of the new physics, Descartes thought he could put an end to the mixture of physical and mental he detected in Aristotelianism, which had been dominant until the sixteenth century. The notion of *aistheton* central to *De anima,* and which would have to be translated as "the sensible,"[45] precedes the distinction of physical perception and mental sensation. Merleau-Ponty, referring to Descartes's famous analogy between vision and a blind man's cane, claims in *Eye and Mind* that "the Cartesian concept of vision is . . . touch" (*OE,* 37/170). More exactly, as he will say in the lecture course on Descartes, it is touch in the sense of "contact" (*NC,* 177). Vision then becomes a purely mechanical procedure, and the topography of perception is constituted by levels of resistance, in accordance with the archetype of the cane gliding over tree roots, stones, and sand.[46] Just as a wall's hardness conditions how a ball bounces,[47] vision is shaped as a function of the opacity of things. No sensible qualities are required for that physicalist explanation, therefore, only quantities such as "length, breadth, and depth."[48] To defend himself against the sixth objection of the theologians, who reproached him for reducing man to a machine, Descartes reintroduced sensation, this time locating it in the human mind and denying it any existence "outside my thought."[49] Every sensible quality must therefore be detached from a relation to the object perceived; instead, it is to be conceived in the same terms as an idea, which, as we know, bears no resemblance to what it designates. Between blind contact and clear and distinct *intuitus mentis,* there is no place for actual vision; perception "in the act" (*OE,* 34/176, trans. modified) can have no place.[50]

In that way, Merleau-Ponty would find in Descartes the source of the dualism underlying the Western tradition, the separation of the phenomenal fabric between two opposing but complementary poles. The contradiction between a world of opaque objects stuffed to capacity and the ethereal strata of a transparent ideality is only apparent. "Philosophy is flattened to the sole plane of ideality or to the sole plane of existence," the only choice remaining being that between "internal adequation of the idea or self-identity of the thing" (*VI,* 166–67/127). Once again, the interdependence of opposites—identified from *The Structure of Behavior* on— manifests itself at the ontological level as well: "This infinite distance, this absolute proximity express in two ways—as a soaring over or as fusion— the same relationship with the thing itself" (*VI,* 166/127). That "same relationship" will establish a unified metaphysics, which Merleau-Ponty also calls a *metaphysics of coincidence* (*VI,* 167/127). To destabilize that philosophy of coincidence, which is blind to the fact that every "vision is tele-vision" (*VI*, 321/273), one would have to return to the ambiguity manifested in the visible: "this idea of proximity through distance" (an idea that already appears in Merleau-Ponty's reflection on language),[51] "of intuition as auscultation or palpation in depth" (*VI*, 168/128). In short, one would have to move beyond a strabic, dual-plane ontology toward an ontology rooted in sensible experience.

But is an ontology of experience truly imaginable? That, at least, is the question Merleau-Ponty asks following a reflection on phenomenological reduction and variation: "In order to really reduce an experience to its essence, we should have to achieve a distance from it that would put it entirely under our gaze, with all the implications of sensoriality or thought that come into play in it, bring it and bring ourselves wholly to the transparency of the imaginary, think it without the support of any ground, in short, withdraw to the bottom of nothingness" (*VI*, 147–48/111). The grasping of essence would entail the possibility of a "total variation" (*VI*, 148/111), which would itself require extracting oneself from any place of belonging and situating oneself within the perspective of nothingness itself. Every be-ing, therefore, would stand out against the ground of a nothingness understood as nonbeing, which would determine every be-ing as positive being. But the thing, thus defined as positivity, self-identity, plenitude, "is not the thing of our experience; it is the image we obtain of it by projecting it into a universe where experience would not be bound to anything, where the spectator would abandon the spectacle—in short, by confronting it with the possibility of nothingness" (*VI*, 213/162, trans. modified). The metaphysics of coincidence would in fact rest on a misuse of the principle of sufficient cause, or, in Leibniz's famous formulation, on the question "Why is there something *rather than nothing*?" Such an inquiry falls under the category of what Bergson would call *pseudo-problems,* the interrogative form masking the fact that, concealed behind the alternative between existence and nothing, is the thesis of a prior nothingness, one that comes *earlier.*[52] Merleau-Ponty draws on Bergson's critique of nothingness in order to distance himself, once more, from Jean-Paul Sartre. Although Sartre also set out to destroy objectivist ontology, in *Being and Nothingness* he remained captive to a positive conception of being, precisely because that notion still rests on the position of a prior nothingness. According to Merleau-Ponty, such a move still involves reversing the proper order, given that no one can have the experience of logical nothingness. On the contrary, "Is not the experience of the thing and of the world precisely the ground that we need in order to think nothingness in any way whatever?" (*VI*, 213/162). We are faced with a strange parallelism between objectivist ontology, justified by a thesis that posits nothingness, and an ontology of nothingness that determines it as a plenitude to which nothing can be added. Between the self-transparency of nothingness and the be-ing's fullness, a metaphysics of overdetermination invites itself on the stage which drags along behind itself an ontology of experience, which we force "to say more than it said" (*VI*, 213/162). To say that nothingness *is not* is still to say too much about it; to posit being is also to bring it back into the company of be-ings, thereby missing its *meaning*. As a result—and this re-mark, from a note of May 1960, is key—any dialectic of Being and Noth-ingness "disregards Being and prefers the object to it" (*VI*, 296/248).

We have seen that any theory of perception can rise above reifying dualisms only by becoming ontology. Conversely, ontology can be only an ontology of the sensible—otherwise, it would contradict its ambition to undo the anthropocentric privilege—since the sensible "is precisely that medium in which there can be *being* without it having to be posited" (*VI*, 262/214). The matter at hand, then, is to conceive a new ontology of the sensible, which Merleau-Ponty, after Valéry, will also call "aesthesiology" (*VI*, 220/168). It will consist of the "unveiling of a Being that is not posited because it has no need to be, because it is silently behind all our affirmations, negations, and even behind all formulated questions" (*VI* 169/129, trans. modified). The Being of the sensible, neither grafted onto nothingness nor plastered onto the world of determinate *qualia,* is riddled with negativity. Sartre "constructs" the union of Being and negativity, but one must rather conceive that sensible Being as always already "shadowed [*doublé*] by noth-ingness" (*VI*, 286/237, trans. modified). In a note dating to May 1960 titled "Visible Invisible," Merleau-Ponty announces: "The sensible, the visible, must be for me the occasion to say what nothingness is" (*VI*, 306/258). Although the tradition attempts to move beyond the constitutive duality by distributing the two orders on different planes, thus producing ontological "strabism," one must rather accept the encroachment of the two orders on each other, within a single perspective.

Merleau-Ponty will designate that encroachment with a term borrowed from Maurice Blondel, *diplopia*.[53] In *L'être et les êtres (Being and Beings),* Blondel postulates that the history of Western ontology has followed two different axes: One ascends from existing beings to Being as essence (on-tological *anabasis*); the other descends (*katabasis*) from essence to existing beings. The beginning of a chapter heading no doubt attracted Merleau-Ponty's attention: "Can our ontological diplopia be brought back to the unity of a binocular vision? And in what way phenomenology is not suf-ficient for founding ontology."[54] An immediate echo can be found in one of Merleau-Ponty's course descriptions: "Could we not find what has been called an 'ontological diplopia' (Blondel), which after so much philosophical effort we cannot expect to bring to a rational reduction and which leaves us with the sole alternative of wholly embracing it, just as our gaze takes over monocular images to make a single vision out of them" (*RC*, 127/158, trans. modified). Reformulated in terms of Merleau-Ponty's own horizon, that amounts to saying that the ontology of the visible will have to be combined with a reflection on voids, the holes of latency with which it is pocked, a nothingness that turns out to be more than a purely logical category: a nothingness of this world, inserted into the visible as its underside, since "nothingness is nothing more (nor less) than the invisible" (*VI*, 306/258).

Merleau-Ponty adds, however, that we must not conceive of that invisibility as a nonvisibility added onto the visible, an objectivity that is simply *elsewhere*: "The invisible is not another visible ('possible' in the logical sense) a positive only *absent*" (*VI*, 300/251). Beyond Husserl's unresolved dualism between *Urpräsenz* (primal presence) and *Appräsenz* (derived presence), one must describe "a certain relation between the visible and the invisible, where the invisible is not only non-visible (what has been or will be seen and is not seen, or what is seen by an other than me, not by me), but where its absence counts in the world (it is 'behind' the visible, imminent or eminent visibility, it is *Urpräsentiert* precisely as *Nichturpräsentierbar*, as another dimension) where the lacuna that marks its place is one of the points of passage of the 'world'" (*VI*, 277/228).

Conclusion: Toward Dia-Phenomenology

Being-at-a-Distance

A philosophy that was abruptly cut short by the death of its author cannot be criticized for being inconclusive. But there has often been too great a tendency to see the suspension of Merleau-Ponty's oeuvre as the ultimate expression of a mode of thought whose strength would lie entirely in its incompletion. Twenty years after the philosopher's passing, Michel de Certeau summed up the fascination of *The Visible and the Invisible* as a petrified fragment of thought: "Like the mineralized bodies at Pompeii, it bears the inscribed record of the double quake that shook it: an ontological passion and the death that interrupted its gesture."[1]

As inchoate as the effect of such an incompletion may be for the interpreter's thinking, as galvanizing the study of scattered notes that do not yet constitute yet a "work," we must not lose sight of the fact that these notes correspond to a very precise imperative on their author's part. Merleau-Ponty's aversion for decisive gestures is well known. "In philosophy," he said, "as soon as you judge that a philosophy is expressed sufficiently in its concluding sentence, well then, you have fallen into barbarism" (*DE*, July 3, 1959, interview 7, "L'existentialisme athée"). And the idea of a philosophy as linguistic therapy, which would consist primarily of dissolving what can only be considered false problems, was clearly at odds with his way of thinking. Nevertheless, his rejection of any conclusion does not mean that there is no methodological imperative, traces of which can be detected throughout his oeuvre. It is this imperative, but, even more than that, the coherence of the means implemented to realize it, that must be put to the critical test in order to determine—beyond commonplaces and rote formulas—what Merleau-Ponty's legacy at the time of his death really was.

I have shown that the later Merleau-Ponty strove to undo the one-size-fits-all categories that lead endlessly back to dichotomies, and to accede to a philosophy of intertwining and chiasms, a philosophy defined as a rejection of the instruments that either empirical intuition or conceptual thinking have provided. In short, his philosophy sought to install itself "in a locus where they have not yet been distinguished" (*VI*, 170/130). Merleau-Ponty, following the precept that we must seek "to form our first concepts in such a way as to avoid the classical impasses" (*VI*, 178/137), introduced into philosophy expressions that now bear his signature, such as "dimensionality," "verticality," "framing" (*membrure*), "hinge," "encroachment," "insistent Being" (*Être de prégnance*), and so on. Nevertheless, the working notes—only about half of which were published by Claude Lefort in *The Visible and the Invisible*—convey the difficulties in setting up a new framework, in providing a new groundwork for these expressions. If, to avoid the pitfalls of intuitionism and empiricism, a philosophy of experience must become an ontology, that ontology will have to be rigorously conceived as being rooted in the sensible.

As I noted at the beginning of this book, in 1948 Merleau-Ponty began his radio lecture series known as *The World of Perception* by saying that the "perceptual world" remains in large part unknown territory, ignored both in the philosophical tradition and in utilitarian attitudes. That world is furnished with countless sensible things that we handle on a daily basis, that we perceive, hear, feel, and taste, and that are rarely the object of a particular reflection: They are there, in all their sensorial presence, as so many invitations to be put to use, in accordance with the finality that the moment and context would choose to confer on them. Ultimately, however, the utilitarian attitude dovetails with intellectualism, which is characteristic of the philosophical anthropocentrism when it considers these objects only as transitional objects, the finality of which justifies their existence.

But then, what would it mean to consider sensible objects not only as transitive signs or vectors that guarantee a practical or epistemological utility but also as things that, by virtue of their materiality and texture, have a consistency specific to them and resist being grasped without any remainder? What would it mean to learn to see the world anew, in the full and exacting sense of the term—in other words, to use our sensibility to approach a world that is in its turn conditioned by its sensible being? What does the famous "return to the things themselves" called for by phenomenology consist of? In a sense, obviously, the entire philosophical enterprise has consisted of seeking a privileged mode of access to things, by determining their substantial being and attaining true knowledge of them. According to Merleau-Ponty, however, learning to see the world anew must entail, in the first place, unlearning what we believed we knew. To return to the things themselves, he writes in the preface to *Phenomenology of Perception,* is to return to "this world prior to knowledge, this world of which knowledge always *speaks*" (*PP*, iii/lxxii). If, then, there is reason to privilege the "perceptual situation," it is not so much to reverse the metaphysical tropism from eternal objects (God or the geometric figure) to objects of sensation as it is to insist on the sensible condition of any relationship to objects. That is the problem on which any enterprise that attempts to ground the autonomy of the external world founders.

To say that a sensible object possesses attributes, such as number or extension, independent of any observer, and that there are therefore primary qualities with an autonomous existence apart from phenomenal qualities (*qualia,* or secondary qualities) does not guarantee exteriority: on the contrary. Paradoxically, instead of affirming the object's autonomy, such a claim, in defining exhaustively the object by the properties attributed to it, only brings it closer to the orbit of consciousness. Indeed, though the aim of that "objective" determination is to determine the object independent of its modes of giving, it ends up falling into the worst sort of relativism, since it reduces objects that are unique each time to "systems of transparent relationships," formalizable for a consciousness to which nothing is ever alien because it never has anything alien within it. We must resign ourselves: An object defined in its entirety will not be more objective. Rather, it will lose what makes the object what it is, in other words, the fact of being *ob-iectum,* thrown across, since the movement that grounds all experience will have been arrested. In that respect, it is clear why taking things as "identifiable nuclei . . . we arrive at the thing-object, at the in-itself, at the thing identical with itself, only by imposing upon experience an abstract dilemma unknown to it" (*VI*, 212/162, trans. modified). The thing thus defined is reduced to a figure without ground, floating in a bottomless void; rather than a thing, it is the simulacrum of a thing, the "image we obtain of it by projecting it into a universe where experience would not be bound to anything" (*VI*, 213/162, trans. modified). The more disconnected exteriority is from any correlation, the more, it seems, it settles in as a product of the mind. Seen from that angle, the lesson of Merleau-Ponty remains salutary, at a time when contemporary philosophy—like pre-Kantian philosophy back in the day—is again tempted to posit an absolute Outside. Let's face it: Nothing is more anthropological than an in-itself, given that the in-itself is nothing but an "in-itself for us" (*PP*, 372/336).

Vis-à-vis this philosophical tradition, Merleau-Ponty brings about two decisive displacements. In the first place, he ceases to define the perceptual object in terms of exteriority and henceforth determines it by its distance. That amounts to saying that *sensible being is being-at-a-distance*, in every sense of the word: distance as the opposite of proximity (but still synonymous with an irreducible gap, the condition of experience) but also distance as an obstacle to the grasping of being with no remainder. The sensible object is thus not an absolutely *transcendent* object: "Being-at-a-distance of the perceived—it is not transcendent, since on principle there can be no question of positing it outside of its distance, *in itself* or *for itself*" (MBN 8.2, fol. 72b). In the second place, Merleau-Ponty modifies what might have been only a logical determination of distance. Being-at-a-distance cannot be reduced to a new figure for the *transcendental*, the formal condition of possibility for any appearing. Rather, the phenomenological ontology outlined in his last manuscripts is akin to a material ontology, inasmuch as the space between things does not so much constitute a pure form of understanding as it corresponds to a milieu, to which Merleau-Ponty wants to restore a density proper. Everything that is sensible belongs to "the common fabric of which we are made. Wild Being" (*VI*, 253/203, trans. modified). The frequent invocation of what he calls "wild Being" or "brute Being" must therefore be understood as the rejection both of an objective ontology and of a formal cosmology. What is "brute" is coarse, unpolished, resistant, but also basic, fundamental, elementary.

One of the horizons of which Merleau-Ponty's last working notes provide us a glimpse is precisely an exploration of the elementary, but not in the sense of an original chemistry of things, as a list of their components, or of a first alphabet. Rather, "element" takes on the sense given that term by the pre-Socratics: indivisible and yet shared, sensible but without ever being the object of a perception. To consider such an element an individual be-ing would be inadequate, whereas to call it "Being" in the Heideggerian sense would be too much. If, says Merleau-Ponty, we are to revive "the old term 'element,' in the sense it was used to speak of water, air, earth, and fire," we must understand it "in the sense of a *general thing*, midway between the spatiotemporal individual and the idea, a sort of incarnate principle that brings a style of being wherever there is a fragment of being" (*VI*, 182/139). The element—or rather, the elements, since, like the elements of the ancients, they are always plural, as Gaston Bachelard noted—the elements, then, as Merleau-Ponty explains, are "not objects, but fields" (*VI*, 314/267). Hence the perceptual situation, the philosophical anchorage Merleau-Ponty provides for himself, is never abandoned but is rather radicalized in its presuppositions. On the model of vision and the visual field, he will call an "element" that which, within the sensible, produces a field effect, spaces things, both distributes them and connects them to one another. The field, without ever being objectifiable (since it is the condition for an object's appearing), is, however, not insensible; it is perceptible indirectly, like a dominant color that backlights what is deployed against the ground, or like a style imprinted on things.

Oblivion of the Sensible

In the twentieth century, many philosophies called for a return to the concrete, to things. It goes without saying that each of the sciences whose method these philosophies call into question would claim to be doing precisely that, that is, providing concrete access to objects. But in assuming the obviousness of objects—such is the critique formulated by Husserl—the sciences assume, precisely, something *before* things that is never questioned, since the *explanandum* is quite simply replaced by the *explanans*. Under what conditions do things become objects? What ensures their obviousness? All in all, Husserl will say, it is the exclusive focus on things that makes them become distant, inasmuch as decontextualization—a necessary condition for establishing their invariance—reduces them to mere ideas of things. There is thus a forgetting—an oblivion—of things that results from an oblivion of their situation, in other words, of the loci of experience, which, precisely, guaranteed that the things were more than mere abstractions. Husserl arrives at an astonishing conclusion: The oblivion of things, he says, results from an oblivion of the "milieu of intuition" (*anschauliche Umwelt*) and an "oblivion of the subjective" (*Vergessen des Subjektiven*).[2] According to Husserl, the return to things must entail in the first place a reduction to the modes by which they give themselves to a consciousness. That explains why many phenomenologists after Husserl believed that this attempt to rescue things actually imprisoned them within the thick walls of subjectivism and never answered the question of the ontological status of these phenomena. Heidegger will therefore counter Husserl's *oblivion of the subjective* with his diagnosis of the *oblivion of Being*.

Although Merleau-Ponty clearly retains elements of both Husserl and Heidegger in his effort to rebuild phenomenology on the foundation of an ontology of the sensible, he identifies a risk of abstraction in both their procedures: in the direction of a transcendental ego in Husserl's case, in that of an anonymous Being in Heidegger's. To protect oneself from that risk, Merleau-Ponty holds, one would have to start again from a different kind of oblivion, the "oblivion of the sensible." By this expression, Merleau-Ponty does not mean the traditional denigration of which the sense faculties have been the object in philosophy or the traditional "contempt of the body," to use Nietzsche's expression. After all, it would not be impossible to remedy that kind of oblivion, by developing, for example, a philosophy of the body. In that case, *Phenomenology of Perception* would be situated in the direct line of a Nietzschean rehabilitation of the body and its powers, which are the seat of the "big reason," in opposition to the "little reason" of the mind. But when Merleau-Ponty's later manuscripts evoke an "oblivion of the sensible," they do not do so as a lack that some doctrine might be able to fill. At issue is an irreducible oblivion, an imperception within every perception, which corresponds to a constitutive "ignorance" (*VI*, 247/197). That is why "nothing is more difficult than knowing precisely *what we see*," since we are faced with a certain dialectic by virtue of which "perception hides itself from itself" (*PP*, 71/59). It is truly because there is an oblivion of the field that a particular object can appear against its ground in a determinate manner, in one or another of its aspects, and so on. We arrive at the paradoxical conclusion that the "obviousness of the sensible" turns out to be synonymous with an "oblivion of the sensible" (MBN 6, fol. 241). That gives us a better grasp of why perception is diacritical in nature: It produces distinction and indistinction at once. It pulls us toward the *explicatio* while generating concurrently *im-plicatio* ("perception as differentiation, forgetting [*oubli*] as undifferentiation" [*VI*, 247/197]). The structure of the field, with the polarity between its thematic focal point and its indistinct periphery, is called upon to revise the classic notion of the transcendental. Instead of a logical condition that precedes experience, what is at issue is a "transcendental field" that is, so to speak, immanent to the experience it structures. As a result, and because of its very character, which is in its turn partial and limited, there is no decontextualizable and universalizable transcendental. Merleau-Ponty, not content to downsize the universalizing ambitions of transcendental philosophy—an inclination he shares with other twentieth-century thinkers—draws further conclusions from the notion of "transcendental field." Up to his last unpublished writings, he always conceives of the ontological field in terms of its Gestaltist nature.[3] For him, therefore, it is not enough to state, as Heidegger does, that all meaning unfolds within a horizon of signification that is inevitably finite. Meaning is never completely dissociable from its sensible inscription. Fields of meaning ought therefore to be conceived in terms of their sensible element, which, for want of appearing itself, shines through [*transparaît*] what it arranges and articulates.

In insisting on the irreducibly sensible dimension of all meaning (and hence its singular, embedded, embodied, situated dimension) and on the chiasmatic relationship that exists between the sensible and sense, Merleau-Ponty marks out a position halfway between two tendencies often observed in phenomenology: to collapse the meaning of phenomena either to a constitutive subjectivity or, conversely, to an entity "behind" phenomena (the World, Nature, Being). Merleau-Ponty calls that tendency the "strabism of phenomenology," already apparent in Husserl himself, when he seems to hesitate between an absolute consciousness and an all-encompassing Nature that precedes consciousness (*N*, 103–4/72).

Merleau-Ponty, then, is clearly attentive to that methodological problem and warns more than once against the temptation to resolve the encroachment of things in one direction or the other and to dissolve the fabric of the sensible, "this fine-grained texture which stops exploration" (*SG*, 211/167, trans. modified), into something more fundamental, to reduce it to a principle. These are all ways of not taking into account the embeddedness of experience, the fact that what appears is indissociable from a certain element that constitutes its field. (This is a very old epistemological problem, dating back to the Ionian philosophers, each of whom could not resist, in their endorsement of the elements, designating one as more fundamental than all the others and from which they were supposedly derived: for Anaximenes, air; for Thales, water; for Heraclitus, fire; and so on.)

The question that remains open to this day—and rightly so—is whether Merleau-Ponty himself avoided the pitfalls he had pointed out, namely, analytical "strabism" and the temptation of the originary. Granted, there will never be a satisfactory answer to that question, because of the incompletion of his oeuvre. Nonetheless, a greater attention to the posthumous texts that have come to light in the last few years will allow us to move beyond the cleavage between simplistic condemnation and apologetics that has long characterized attitudes toward Merleau-Ponty. In any case, the last texts express a constant hesitation, and any commentator would be well advised to consider these internal, sometimes contradictory movements for what they are.

It has been argued that Merleau-Ponty, inclined to favor a subjective explanation of the oblivion of the sensible in the first period of his oeuvre, made a clear shift in the last phase, toward an explanation to be sought in the world itself. Indeed, the very structure of the world seems to provide a perfect explanation for the phenomenon of oblivion: The world, as phenomenology describes it, does not comprise the totality of be-ings but rather serves as a general horizon. Things give themselves to be sensed, touched, understood, against the ground of the world, which never appears on its own. Merleau-Ponty's later philosophy would thus come close to a *cosmo-logy* (in the literal sense of the term, that is, a philosophy of the world). And in fact, his move from an insistence on the embodied subject to the "flesh of the world" would seem to validate such a reading. A reorientation of that type inevitably leads to a reinterpretation of what preceded, and it becomes impossible to see the expression "flesh of the world" as a sort of generalization of bodily structures (see the section titled "Ontology of the Flesh" in chapter 3 above), which would now extend to the world as a whole: "The 'flesh of the world' is not [a] metaphor of our worldly body. One could put this the other way round: it's rather our body that is made of the same sensible stuff that the world is made of" (*NC*, 211). In this scenario, one can no longer say that our being in the world results from our having a body; rather, it is by virtue of our being in the world, which entails being made of a certain sensible stuff, that one can say we have a body.

If that interpretation is correct, it simply marks a reversal in perspective: Whereas Husserl had insisted on the *Leib* as "one's own body," which is to say, as a body that, unlike objective external bodies, is a body that belongs only to oneself, Merleau-Ponty's idea of a flesh of the world now emphasizes that one belongs to an exteriority extending beyond the realm of subjectivity. The invocation of the body and of flesh would then have served only to justify two respective forms of belonging. I certainly have no intention of arguing that the question of belonging is not decisive for philosophy. Indeed, in the transition from "one's own body" as Husserl understands it to the notion of "flesh," what is at stake is the separation of the notion of belonging from the dimension of "ownness," of property: To belong to a world is obviously not to be among the properties of the world but rather to inhere in a world. No modelization, no generalization, no de-contextualization (whether in the sciences or in a literary fiction) will be able to erase altogether one's original context, one's historical, cultural, technical, or ideological dependency. To insist on an inherence in what is thus entails resisting the dream of a transparent grasp of things, which would appear as they are, in their being, autonomous and pure, freed from all the moorings that tied them to contingent contexts. That is why, when Merleau-Ponty invokes an "ontology of the inside," that expression means the exact opposite of an exclusion of the outside. By "inside," we must understand, not a regression of sorts to the internal or visceral depths of oneself, but rather embeddedness in a field. *Being* is always being-at-a-distance and simultaneously *being in*.

That explains the remarkable reversal of the term "narcissism" brought about by Merleau-Ponty: To say that every act of vision is narcissistic is not, in fact, to emphasize internal reflexivity (that is, the fact that any consciousness of something is also a self-consciousness, and that, in perceiving, we perceive ourselves in the act of perceiving). It is rather the reverse. When Merleau-Ponty explains that the self is a self "by virtue of confusion, narcissism, inherence of the one who sees in the seen, of the one who touches in the touched" (OE, 18–19/124, trans. modified), what is at issue is precisely a transindividuality. By definition, a sentient being is also potentially a sensed being (to have a body entails not only the possibility of seeing but also that of being exposed to the gaze in return), and our sensibility can thus be directed only toward things that share our own ontological structure. In opposition to philosophies that affirm rather too quickly the autonomy of the sensible, without explaining where and in what bodies that sensible is experienced, Merleau-Ponty thus allows us to better clarify the ontological conditions of sensibility, as a dimension situated beyond the alternatives of activity and passivity. That dimension is not so much a sense faculty for which I would possess the initiative as a power to which I belong and which grasps me as much as I seize hold of it (just as it seizes all the other forms of life, which will also be defined by their sensibility). Furthermore, even the voyeur—that figure so brilliantly analyzed by Sartre—whose particularity lies precisely in the attempt to break away from that reciprocity between the one seeing and the seen, and who is eventually recaptured by the sense of shame and put on trial by an internal observer, only confirms that correlation in spite of himself.[4]

Whereas the notion of flesh emphasizes *inherence,* that of vision underscores the *spacing* necessary in any sensible relationship. That may partly explain the strange privilege granted to the visual realm in Merleau-Ponty's last major work, whose working title, as mentioned, was *The Visible and the Invisible* (and not *The Touchable and the Untouchable* or, quite simply, *The Sensible and the Insensible*). It is as if he needed to insist on the irreducible distance, on everything that resists a complete and homogeneous resorption, on the opening produced by any act of vision and which, he says, corresponds to a "fission of Being" (OE, 81/186), a dehiscence, a permanent reversal, where the Other is transformed into the Same and the Same into the Other, without there ever being a stable state. There is nothing of that in the term "flesh of the world," however, and Merleau-Ponty seems himself to have realized as much, when he remarks that "the flesh of the world is not self-sensing [*se sentir*] as is my flesh—It is sensible and not sentient" (VI, 304/250). All things considered, to insist so much on belonging to the world (on the fact, therefore, that the expression "vision of the world" is always a subjective genitive, that vision is always the world's vision, a vision proper to the world), is to lose, precisely, that reversibility, that fundamental instability of the sensible, which must always be understood simultaneously "in the twofold sense of what one senses and what senses" (*VI*, 307/259). It is as if the cosmological turn ended up seriously compromising the principle of reversibility, which Merleau-Ponty, let us remember, had made the "ultimate truth" (*VI*, 155/204). (That reversibility is precisely not symmetrical but stems from an incompressible time lag.) When Merleau-Ponty seems tempted to unify the polyperspectivism he had brought to light, by positing something like a unified flesh of the world and Being as the "element of elements" (*NC*, 131), there is reason to doubt that this is a conceptual advance.

Many therefore opt to retain only a "light" version of that late project of an ontology of the sensible: Merleau-Ponty's critique of any godlike position located above it all and of any attempt to isolate things, his emphasis on the indissociable connection that things maintain with the field in which they appear. Granted, it was not the least of Merleau-Ponty's contributions to contemporary philosophy to have insisted on that inscription—which is also always an opening—to have insisted, that is, on the inherence in distance and the distance in inherence. In fact, that insight tallies with the conclusions of other important theoretical movements of the twentieth century, both continental hermeneutics and post-Wittgensteinian pragmatics, which point out that the meaning of something can be identified only in relation to a particular context of signification, to one or another field of usages or referential horizon.

Yet the late manuscripts clearly contain further avenues for reflection, beyond that insistence on the irreducible plurality and contextuality of all meaning. There are in these texts the premises of a philosophy that emphasizes not only inherence and difference but also the intrinsically operative dimension of what is. And it is possible, as I will try to argue, to glimpse in those premises a new way of conceiving the phenomenological project as such.

Toward Dia-Phenomenology

How does our perception work? What do we see each time that we see? What is the nature of what we touch, taste, and hear, and how is that experience possible? This inquiry, as already noted, haunts Merleau-Ponty's entire oeuvre. In the last texts, something of an answer emerges, one that allows us to reformulate the question in the wake of a displacement from the ontology of the object to an ontology of the element. Let us return to the beginning: For Merleau-Ponty, as for Husserl, sensible experience teaches us something essential, namely, that the sensible object as it gives itself in experience is indissociable from its phenomenal suchness. It is impossible to visualize a sound, a landscape, or a path in general; these things will always have a particular form, a singular aspect, a certain timbre, an actual material quality, a given affective coloration. Nonetheless, though there is no sound or color in general, there is a generality of sound and a generality of color. By "generality," Merleau-Ponty does not mean universality, in the sense that every occurrence of color would represent a token of a universal type (somewhat like a color you might choose to paint a wall from a color chart provided by a paint dealer), but rather the fact that the singular occurrence always already gestures toward something beyond itself, toward something transversal. Color "surpasses itself of itself: as soon as it becomes colored lighting, the dominant color of the field" (*VI*, 271/217, trans. modified). If the sensible being is thus indissociable from its being-so, the partial modality of any giving already signals toward other modalities that are currently absent. As a result, one would have to rethink generality as something that is "not above" but "beneath," "not before, but *behind* us" (*VI*, 272/218).

Two avenues open up here: first, that of an *eidetic phenomenology*, and second, that of a *revised theory of the universal*. The aim of eidetic phenomenology is to draw out the essence of things beyond their individual variations. From that standpoint, Merleau-Ponty's strength would consist not so much in emphasizing the difference between occurrences (Husserl's *Tatsachen,* or facts), which are always arbitrary, and the invariant essence (Husserl's *Wesen*), but in showing that the only eidetic phenomenology is an operative phenomenology, in other words, one operating by *means of* and *through* the variations. In that sense, the invariance of a thing (the Holy Grail that philosophy has been searching for since Plato) is not what is "absent from every bouquet," to speak like the poet Stéphane Mallarmé; rather, it exists only amid the variations themselves. It is therefore possible to maintain that "the invariant, since it is grasped only *through variation,* is to the variants (= the 'gaps') what the 'mobile' is to 'movement'" (*MPR*, 444/445, trans. modified). The invariant is not a positive term, of which movement would be an attribute or a property; it is rather what can be detected negatively *through* movement. There is no essence as ground or substance: The *eidos* is what, in exceeding singular phenomenalizations, persists through them.

But Merleau-Ponty does not merely indicate a new way of apprehending eidetic analysis: He also advances toward a *revised theory of the universal*. In other words, not content to insist on the necessity of thinking being on the basis of the being-so, he wonders whether there is something like a being of suchness, a generality of the "what it is like." It is on this point that the working notes contain interesting possibilities. To concede that the essence of a thing is not what one grasps *despite* its occurrences, which are always partial, but rather *through* them, is to say that modality precedes essence. Merleau-Ponty echoes that intuition when he advances this hypothesis: "Perception is not in the first place the perception of things but of *elements* (water, air), *rays of the world,* things which are dimensions, which are worlds; I slide over these 'elements,' and there I am in the *world*" (*VI*, 267/218, trans. modified).

This is a spectacular reversal of Husserl's thesis of intentionality, since for Husserl, obviously, perceptual intentionality is an object-oriented intentionality: I hear not a whistling but the teakettle that tells me the water is boiling; I perceive not a mass of colored blotches but my friend advancing toward me in the street. What does it mean, then, to affirm that the element is primary in relation to the object? Granted, the element is sensible—just as a visual field, a sound environment, or an olfactory atmosphere may be—but it is obviously not perceptible in the same way as an object. It requires a specific operation to visualize the spacing between things; one can thematize as an object what is simply a transitive element, but only at the cost of losing the transitivity that made it operative. That is the reason one never paints a color but always only *something* colored, just as one cannot depict the content of a sensation, a sound in itself, and so on.

We may therefore wonder whether Merleau-Ponty is really correct when he says that we perceive the element before the thing. The example of atmosphere seems to indicate otherwise. One never penetrates an atmosphere; one senses its quality only after the fact (for example, when, having joined a meeting already in progress, one perceives there is a storm brewing). One does not perceive an atmosphere the way one would perceive an object: What is missing is the familiar shape of the thing. One perceives an atmosphere indirectly—one breathes it in more than one conceives it; one perceives in accord with it, *through it.*

All these problems indicate one of the major impasses in Merleau-Ponty's late manuscripts. The project of an ontology of the elements appears to be pulled in two different directions at once: toward a phenomenological cosmology, like the one that the Czech phenomenologist Jan Patočka proposed, for example, and toward a phenomenology of fields, which, however, does not manage to rid itself of the eidetic model. It is as if the field were only the background of an object, as if one had only to turn one's attention away from the objects and toward the space between them to understand what produces their appearance. But experimental psychology has demonstrated that, when one shifts one's gaze from the focal area to the margins, the paradigm of objectification is not thereby undone. When I turn my attention to the margins, they cease to be margins and become the object in turn, surrounded by new margins. It is a struggle, in any event, to glimpse a synthesis in Merleau-Ponty's thinking between his concern for a rigorous elucidation, in the direct line of his earliest analyses, and a certain mysticism of the ineffable—one has only to think of the evocation of Schelling's "barbaric principle" (*VI*, 315/267), of the "polymorphic matrix" of Being (*VI*, 274/221), of the return of flesh to a maternal womb ("flesh, the mother") (*VI*, 321/267). The metaphysical temptation seems unavoidable: In addition to showing why all perception entails a nonperception, why every instance of vision has a blind spot, a *punctum caecum,* he vests that purely structural determination with a metaphysical value. The invisible aspect of any visual field is nominalized, becoming, as it were, the Invisible of the world (*VI*, 196/151), what is "absent from all flesh" (*VI*, 198/151).

There is reason to ask whether Merleau-Ponty, mired in these methodological dilemmas, was quite simply unable to pursue to its conclusion his intuition of an ontology of the sensible as a phenomenology of the elements. One thing is certain: It is neither through a generalization of the notion of flesh nor through a metaphysics of the invisible that this question that keeps surfacing throughout Merleau-Ponty's entire oeuvre—How is it that there is something in sensible experience rather than nothing?—can finally be solved. The notion of the invisible emphasizes that all experience entails a withdrawing, and the notion of flesh allows us to take into account the reciprocal involvement of the sensing and the sensed, but neither one explains how a mode of appearing comes about that cannot be reduced either to *what* appears or to *the one to whom* it appears. The Greeks had quite a precise expression for everything that shows itself: *phainestai,* which roughly covers what we would call "phenomena." It is noteworthy that *phainestai,* which is used in perfectly everyday contexts ("it appears that," "it seems," "that appears obvious," and so on), is always in the middle voice, a grammatical form that modern European languages have lost, located between the active and the passive. According to Aristotle, philosophy must avoid both dogmatism and skepticism by taking seriously what appears in broad daylight, and must thereby restore the legitimate place of appearances in the wake of Plato's critiques. That is a way of undertaking the "rescue of phenomena" (*sozein ta phainomena*), to which post-Nietzschean philosophy would return in its own way.

Transphenomenality: Aristotle's Intuition

Merleau-Ponty emphasized the importance, for a philosophy closer to sensible appearances (*NC*, 371), of the middle voice, the *vox media*. As it happens, he did not see the proximity between his own philosophy of the sensible and Aristotle's psychology, noting several times that he was not well acquainted with the author of *On the Soul* ("I'm not a great Aristotelian" [*MPR*, 208]). In Aristotle's treatise, he would have found that a great attention was devoted to the sense faculties of the soul, to living organisms, and to the category of the middle voice. Above all, he would have found a very developed conceptualization of a problem that remains only virtual in his own oeuvre: that of the perceptual milieu. A passage from *Eye and Mind* alludes to a philosophical scene that was obviously a decisive event for the author. It concerns an intuition he had on the terrace of the house in Le Tholonet, France, near Aix-en-Provence, in summer 1960:

> When through the water's thickness I see the tiling at the bottom of a pool, I do not see it *despite* the water and the reflections there; I see it through them and because of them. If there were no distortions, no ripples of sunlight, if it were without this flesh that I saw the geometry of the tiling, then I would cease to see it *as* it is and where it is—which is to say, beyond any identical, specific place. I cannot say that the water itself—the aqueous power, the syrupy and shimmering element—is in space; it is not somewhere else either, but it is not in the pool. It inhabits it, it materializes itself there, yet it is not contained there; and if I raise my eyes toward the screen of cypresses where the web of reflections is playing, I cannot gainsay the fact that the water visits it, too, or at least sends into it, upon it, its active and living essence. (*OE*, 70–71/182, trans. modified)

Water and air thus become media that, while nonthematic in the visible, nonetheless pertain to it; as diaphanous elements, they allow something that belongs to the visible without being actually visible in their own right. Merleau-Ponty, without suspecting it, is as close as possible here to the theory of perception laid out by Aristotle. According to that theory, developed in *On the Soul* and in the brief treatises on natural history—the so-called *Parva naturalia*, which had a very particular reception in the Middle Ages and Renaissance—there is no pure appearing. Every *phainestai* requires a milieu in which it appears.[5]

Aristotle, conceiving perception as both an activity and a structure, situates the *medium* at the heart of structure. For him, there is sensation only where a perceptual space, which he calls *metaxy* (medium or intermediary), extends between the sense organ and the sensed object. Breaking ranks with his predecessors, Aristotle opens the way for a thematization of what could be called the *phenomenal milieu,* the space where the genesis of phenomena comes about, through the relation between the sensing body, agent bodies, and sensed qualities. Every sensorial perception occurs in an element such as air or water, and these elements possess certain characteristics that allow them to operate as sensible intermediaries. For example, air may serve as a milieu for hearing, smell, and vision, whereas water is solely a medium for vision. Sensation occurs not so much *in* a milieu as through it or, to use the Greek prefix, *dia.* An element that lets sound pass through will be called *diechēs* (from *dia-echō,* "sounding through"); an element that transmits an odor will be called *diosmōn* (from *dia-osmē*: "smelling through"); and so on. But how to characterize what allows the visible to pass through, what allows it to appear (*phainestai*)?

Aristotle then invents a new concept, that of trans-appearance. What appears does not appear purely and simply to the eye; it appears through a milieu, which Aristotle calls *diaphanous* (from *dia-phanēs,* "visible through"). That operative medium is both the perceptual milieu of vision and the structure of visibility. This notion accounts for the remarkable structure of visual perception itself, in that it cannot occur without combining distance and continuity, cannot forgo a paradoxical form of relationship operating between beings. If there were total continuity between beings, no experience would be possible; only where there is a certain spacing between them can experience occur. Hence the need for a mediating milieu. In Aristotle's description of it, the diaphanous milieu has two different states: a potential and an actual state. In its merely potential state, the diaphanous milieu is perfectly transparent, and one can see through it; when actualizing its capacity, it takes over the visual form of the sensible object and "likens" itself to it. The diaphanous then literally corresponds to a *transformer*: It adopts the form of something (its outer appearance, its *eidos,* stripped of any matter) only to transmit it across distances, all the way to a sense organ. For such a transformative-translational act to take place, the milieu has to feature certain characteristics. The milieu, in order to take a form, must therefore be indeterminate (formless) and must at the same time exhibit a certain density or "texture" (*plexis*),[6] which guarantees its plasticity. Empty space is not only a pure ideality, but, as Aristotle explains, if the space were empty, "not merely would accurate vision be impossible, but nothing would be seen at all."[7] Just as Kant's dove cannot fly in empty space, so can there be no vision without a certain resistance of the medium, which indicates its capacity to be moved.

That intermediary, however, which in perception allows us to touch things, is itself untouchable, invisible, or simply "anesthetic" as it were. The sensible medium will operate all the better inasmuch as, in the aesthesiological experience, what allows for experience vanishes behind what it institutes. Or, to put it more concretely: I cannot touch the air around me; I cannot make it a tangible object. In all sensible experience, therefore, there is an *oblivion of the "between."* The perceptual milieu is, by its very nature, imperceptible, and it is only on the condition that it remain imperceptible that perception operates within it. To characterize the imperceptible nature of the medium, Aristotle uses the verb *lanthanei*, which also means "to forget." What is forgotten is in the background; it remains inapparent. By extension, one can say that we forget the sensible milieu that surrounds us.[8] The greatest distance is lodged in the closest proximity.

An Operative Phenomenology

How to make use of Merleau-Ponty's writings today? They can, of course, be seen as an effective remedy for the marginalization of the embodied and situated dimension of knowledge, and that would not be the least of its merits. But his insistence on the "oblivion of the sensible" can also be interpreted differently. Granted, since the minor seismic event of deconstruction, any reference to the sensible as the source of a primary self-evidence appears suspect, if not naïve, since it seems irremediably to lead back to a metaphysics of presence, as Jacques Derrida would have it. It remains to be proven, however, whether the sensible really is on the side of presence and ideality on the side of absence. Undeniably, when Husserl defines *Leib*, "one's own body," as "presence in person" (*Leibhaftigkeit*), in contrast to what is only "appresented," everything suggests that phenomenology is repeating the traditional metaphysical cleavage between presence and absence. But is one's own body (*Leib*) truly present? Nothing is less certain. For sure, I will never be able to feel someone else's body as I can my own. But can I truly say in turn that my body is *present* to me? Is not the body rather a *vector* of presence, a means of *presentation*, which makes something other than itself appear while it anesthetizes itself in the process? It is not so much that I perceive the body as that I perceive from and through it. As a result, as Merleau-Ponty already said, "to perceive is to render oneself present to something through the body" (*PrP*, 104/42). The body is more than something present: It is *presentative*, and somatic functions will perform their tasks all the better in allowing themselves to be forgotten. Such is the reason that, at this point, *Phenomenology of Perception* invokes a dynamic intentionality that is more "operational" than thematic.

If Merleau-Ponty has now been crowned the philosopher of the body, it is worth rediscovering him as the thinker of the operative, in other words, of all those dimensions of meaning that contribute crucially toward shaping it, even while remaining themselves unperceived. That is why Merleau-Ponty says that the return to "the thing itself" "is not the contrary of mediation" (*SG*, 155/157), and why he can affirm that every thing is nothing but a "mediation of finite and infinite" (MBN 14, fol. 13). The framework of a classic philosophy of representation is definitively abandoned; he is a realist when he says that every relation is a relation to the thing itself and not to its representation. But he also does not confuse realism with immediacy. Just because it is posited that, every time one perceives, desires, or acts, it is the things themselves, and not representations of them, that are perceived, desired, or acted upon, it cannot be deduced therefrom that these things give themselves immediately, in full transparency. All presence is the result of certain conditions of presentation, which we must cease to see merely as neutral backdrops, and whose constitutive operation will have to be described.

Let's just think about it for a moment: Most of the things we have in mind come to us by roundabout means, so to speak. The discovery of the mediated structure of perception would have to be generalized to the sensible world as a whole. We do not perceive sensations; it is *through* them that we perceive. We do not perceive aspects; it is *by means of them* that we grasp the thing. We never possess ourselves entirely; it is through the elements, which we will never to able to elucidate completely, that we have access to ourselves. Just as we did not witness our own birth, we cannot return to ourselves without others who serve as witnesses to what escapes our immediate grasp. Our present situation gives itself through the mediation of memories, personal and intersubjective, and against the ground of a future into which we project ourselves, individually and collectively. The same goes for our finitude, which Heidegger wanted to make into a new "originary." But our own death always comes second; it is other people's deaths that we encounter first. The same is true for the encounter with the Other, which a certain ethical philosophy would like to isolate from any social context. There is no immediacy of the encounter; the encounter with the Other is already "mediated by the relationship with third parties" (*VI*, 112n/81n). So too the norms that govern behaviors: A norm is never directly in front of us—it is not a thing; it is *through it* that social relations are organized, and it is only through these relations that the coherence of the norm shines through. The institution of something unheard-of or unprecedented (a scientific discovery, an artistic creation, a historical revolution) and its profoundly innovative character are perceptible only through the previous state, which one moved through unconsciously and which suddenly appears in broad daylight as past, obsolete, outmoded. Throughout his oeuvre, Merleau-Ponty incessantly pointed out the material circumstances necessary for any revolution: However disruptive the event may be, it is rooted in a specific configuration that makes it emerge. Every creation, however radical, remains a matter of mediation, inasmuch as it discovers, in what is there, the means to leap toward something that no one had been able to see before, because it appeared senseless.

That is another way of returning to the latent potentialities lodged, not so much at the very heart of things, as in the space between them. There is a relationship only by virtue of a medium that connects things and separates them at the same time, a milieu that, rather than being a neutral space, is an operator of spacing. The medium forms a screen of sorts, allowing for something inaccessible or absent to be present, through a presentative operator. In a way, this is the precondition of any vision, as Merleau-Ponty says it very well: "There is no vision without the screen: the ideas we are speaking of would not be better known to us if we had no body and no sensibility; it is then that they would be accessible to us" (*VI*, 194/150). In sum, the medium lets something else appear while making itself forgotten; it visualizes ("aesthetizes") while anesthetizing itself in the process. As a screen for appearances, it offers a receptacle for other beings and a projective space for being other. The act of mediation is indissociable from this alterity and this plastic structure of becoming.

So what to do with Merleau-Ponty today? As time passes, what emerges with increasing clarity is that the path toward the things themselves is full of pitfalls and that to recapture the real it is not enough to proclaim the advent of new object-oriented philosophies. The sensible world cannot be reduced to a set of objects, as the phenomenological critique of the object has demonstrated. What remains to be described is all the complexity of the processes by which things come to appear in their respective fields. Undoubtedly, Merleau-Ponty only glimpsed that phenomenology of the milieus and the media of appearing, and that phenomenology is indisputably more operative than thematic, to borrow Eugen Fink's famous distinction. In a word, it remains a "coming philosophy," one intent on following the multiple ways (epistemological, technical, artistic, political) in which something emerges where, just a moment ago, there seemed to be nothing. These emergences are indissociable from the arrangements that regulate their possibility; and, conversely, at each occurrence, the entire field of what can be said, thought, and seen is reorganized. Philosophy can accompany these processes in turn, can intervene as an operation of sensitization, in both the descriptive and normative senses of that term. Merleau-Ponty said it himself: "The source of meaning is no more behind us than in front of us; it is no more a lost immediacy than an omega point to be reached. . . . It is in the seeing, the speaking, the thinking" (*NC*, 375). In a word, what is at issue is a *sensible practice*.

Notes

Introduction: Return to the Obvious

1. See the list of abbreviations in the frontmatter for all the abbreviations of Merleau-Ponty's works used in the parenthetical references in the text. The first page number is to the text in the French edition, and after the virgule is the page number in the English translation.

2. Edmund Husserl, *Logical Investigations,* ed. Dermot Moran, trans. J. N. Findlay, 2 vols. (London: Routledge, 2001), 2:76.

3. Edmund Husserl, *Husserliana* (hereafter cited in the text as *Hua*), 29:119

4. Plato, *Meno* 80c.

5. Edmund Husserl, *The Crisis of European Sciences and Transcendental Phenomenology,* trans. David Carr (Evanston, Ill.: Northwestern University Press, 1970), 187.

6. Gaston Bachelard, *Earth and Reveries of Will: An Essay on the Imagination of Matter,* trans. Kenneth Haltman (Dallas: Dallas Institute Press, 2002), 39, trans. modified.

7. Plato, *Theaetetus* 155d3.

8. That is why I disagree with Françoise Dastur's reconstruction of Merleau-Ponty as a thinker "of the Inside," as opposed to "thinkers of the Outside" such as Foucault or Blanchot. See Françoise Dastur, "Merleau-Ponty and Thinking from Within," in *Merleau-Ponty in Contemporary Perspective,* ed. Patrick Burke and Jan van Der Veken (Dordrecht: Kluwer, 1993), 25–35.

1. Perception

1. Ludwig Wittgenstein, *Philosophical Investigations,* trans. G. E. M. Anscombe, 3rd ed. (New York: Macmillan, 1958), §107, p. 46.

2. Ibid.

3. See the documents contained in *Le primat de la perception* (*PrP*). I do not subscribe to Theodore Geraets's hypothesis of a break occurring between *The Structure of Behavior* and *Phenomenology of Perception*. See Theodore F. Geraets, *Vers une nouvelle philosophie transcendantale: La genèse de la philosophie de Maurice Merleau-Ponty jusqu'à la Phénoménologie de la Perception,* preface by Emmanuel Levinas (The Hague: Nijhoff, 1971).

4. On this point, see Soraya de Chadarevian, *Zwischen den Diskursen: Merleau-Ponty und die Wissenschaften* (Würzburg: Königshausen & Neumann, 1990), esp. 21–22.

5. That rejection of the "view from above," which will take on its full importance in the late philosophy, is already manifest in Merleau-Ponty's second article on Gabriel Marcel, where the existentialist bias—or even the tendency toward "empiricist mysticism," as Jean Wahl characterized Marcel's thought—stands in contrast to the *intuitus mentis* of the Cartesian subject behind the glass (*P1*, 35–36).

6. For Merleau-Ponty, transparency is above all an optical phenomenon. He discovered its importance for the question of depth of field through the work of Edith Tudor-Hart, whom he cites in his request for research funding (*PrP*, 28/80) and to whom he will devote a few pages in *The Structure of Behavior* (*SC*, 92–93, 97/83, 88). Note that the use of the term in its figurative sense, though generally critical, sometimes tends to fall back into a positive assertion (*SC*, 181/164) in the tradition of philosophical rationalism, which sees transparency as the absence of obstacles to thought.

7. This is a summary of a lecture titled "Structure" that Merleau-Ponty delivered on January 11, 1961. It was first published in the proceedings of the conference, *Sens et usages du terme structure dans les sciences humaines et sociales,* ed. Roger Bastide (The Hague: Mouton, 1962), repr. in *P2*, 317–20.

8. Jakob von Uexküll, *A Foray into the World of Animals and Humans: With a Theory of Meaning,* trans. Joseph D. O'Neill (Minneapolis: University of Minnesota Press, 2010).

9. Kurt Goldstein, *The Organism* (1934), translated from the German (New York: American Book Company, 1939).

10. Léon Brunschvicg, *Les étapes de la philosophie mathémathique* (Paris: Alcan, 1912), 572–73.

11. On the occasion of the fortieth anniversary of his *Cours de philosophie positive* (1838), Auguste Comte introduced that notion, defining it as "the total set of external circumstances . . . necessary for the existence of every determined organism." Auguste Comte, *Philosophie première: Cours de philosophie positive, Leçons 1 à 45,* edited with notes by Michel Serres, François Dagognet, and Allal Sinaceur (Paris: Hermann, 1975), 682.

12. For more details on the history of the concept of milieu, see "The Living and Its Milieu," in Georges Canguilhem, *Knowledge of Life,* trans. Stefanos

Geroulanos and Daniela Ginsburg (New York: Fordham University Press, 2008), 98–120.

13. See Leo Spitzer, "Milieu and Ambiance: An Essay in Historical Semantics," *Philosophy and Phenomenological Research* 3 (September 1942): 1–42, esp. 36.

14. Kurt Koffka, *Principles of Gestalt Psychology* (New York: Harcourt, 1935).

15. Book review of Gabriel Marcel, *Être et avoir,* published in the Catholic review *La Vie Intellectuelle* 45 (October 1936): 98–109 (repr. in *PI*, 35–44).

16. Gabriel Marcel, *Being and Having: An Existential Diary,* translated from the French (New York: Harper & Row, 1966), 11–12.

17. On the idea of virtuality in Merleau-Ponty and a comparison to other theories of the possible and the virtual (in Aristotle, Bergson, Deleuze, and Agamben), see my "The Theatre of the Virtual: How to Stage Potentialities with Merleau-Ponty," in *Encounters in Performance Philosophy,* ed. Laura Cull and Alice Lagaay (Basingstoke: Palgrave Macmillan, 2014), 147–70. For plausible connections to the digital, see Marcello Vitali Rosati, *Corps et virtuel: Itinéraires à partir de Merleau-Ponty* (Paris: L'Harmattan, 2009).

18. On what is at stake for anthropology, see Étienne Bimbenet, *Nature et humanité: Le problème anthropologique dans l'oeuvre de Merleau-Ponty* (Paris: Vrin, 2004).

19. Renaud Barbaras, "Perception et pulsion," *Alter: Revue de Phénoménologie* 9 (2001): 13–26, repr. in his *Vie et intentionnalité—Recherches phénoménologiques* (Paris: Vrin, 2003).

20. See Martin Heidegger, *The Fundamental Concepts of Metaphysics: World, Finitude, Solitude,* trans. William McNeill and Nicholas Walker (Bloomington: Indiana University Press, 1995). In the vast body of literature on the subject, let me mention only Françoise Dastur's "Pour une zoologie privative," *Alter: Revue de Phénoménologie* 3 (1995): 281–317.

21. Goldstein, *Organism,* 87.

22. Ibid., trans. modified.

23. How can we fail to hear an echo of the famous "aids" (*Hülfsmittel*)—the "go-cart" (*Gängelwagen*) and "leading-strings" (*Leitbande*)—in Kant's "Lectures on Pedagogy"? See Immanuel Kant, *Anthropology, History and Education,* trans. Mary Gregor et al. (Cambridge: Cambridge University Press, 2007), 453. In Kant, however, the dichotomy is reestablished in spite of everything: He distinguishes between behavior, determined by the "training apparatus," and the free use of the faculties, oriented toward reason. It is precisely that dichotomy that Merleau-Ponty attempts to break down.

24. Christian Bermes has proposed that we see Merleau-Ponty as the thinker par excellence of mediacy and "mediality": Christian Bermes, "Medialität—Anthropologisches Radikal oder ontologisches Prinzip? Merleau-Pontys Ausführung der Phänomenologie," in *Die Stellung des Menschen in der Kultur: Festschrift für Ernst Wolfgang Orth zum 65. Geburtstag,* ed. Christian Bermes, Julia Jonas, and Karl-Heinz Lembeck (Würzburg: Königshausen & Neumann, 2002), 41–58.

25. Peter Handke, "Essay on Tiredness," in *The Jukebox and Other Essays on Storytelling*, trans. Ralph Manheim and Krishna Winston (New York: Farrar, Straus and Giroux, 1997).

26. Kant returns to it several times, especially in the *Prolegomena to Any Future Metaphysics:* "Transcendental . . . does not mean something that surpasses all possible experience, but something that indeed precedes experience (*a priori*), but that, all the same, is destined to nothing more than solely to make cognition from experience possible." Immanuel Kant, *Prolegomena to Any Future Metaphysics,* ed. and trans. Gary C. Hatfield (Cambridge: Cambridge University Press, 1997), appendix, p. 128n.

27. Does the a priori lend itself to being described not as a logical possibility of experience but as something identifiable in experience itself? Although Ricoeur, Levinas, and Michel Henry, following Merleau-Ponty, each raised that question in his own way, no one has dedicated more attention and importance to it than Mikel Dufrenne, for whom it is in some sense the secret driving force of his thought, from *La notion de l'a priori* (Paris: PUF, 1959; *The Notion of the A Priori*)—where Kant is considered against a phenomenological backdrop—to *L'inventaire des a priori* (Paris: Bourgois, 1981), which Dufrenne considered his philosophical "last will and testament."

28. Edmund Husserl, *Erste Philosophie,* vol. 1: *Kritische Ideengeschichte, Hua (=Husserliana),* 7:280–81.

29. Ibid., 282.

30. Ibid., 281.

31. Jean-Paul Sartre, *The Transcendence of the Ego: An Existentialist Theory of Consciousness,* trans. Forrest Williams and Robert Kirkpatrick (New York: Hill and Wang, 1991), 37.

32. Ibid., 42, trans. modified. On the strange absence/presence of weight in Sartre, I take the liberty of referring to my "Suspension et gravité: L'imaginaire sartrien face au Tintoret," *Alter: Revue de Phénoménologie* 15 (2007): 123–41.

33. Sartre, *Transcendence of the Ego,* 40.

34. See ibid., quotation on p. 98. As we know, this idea will later be developed in *L'être et le néant (Being and Nothingness).*

35. Eugen Fink, "The Phenomenological Philosophy of Edmund Husserl and Contemporary Criticism," in *The Phenomenology of Edmund Husserl: Selected Critical Readings,* ed. R. O. Elveton (Chicago: Quadrangle, 1970), 70–139. The essay is quoted in Merleau-Ponty's first research proposal (1933). See Merleau-Ponty "The Nature of Perception" (*PrP,* 21/77).

36. Fink, "Phenomenological Philosophy of Edmund Husserl," 90.

37. Letter from Heidegger to Husserl, October 22, 1927, in Martin Heidegger, *Becoming Heidegger: On the Trail of His Early Occasional Writings, 1910–1927,* ed. Theodore Kisiel and Thomas Sheehan (Evanston, Ill.: Northwestern University Press, 2007), 237.

38. Merleau-Ponty even had a conversation with Eugen Fink in April 1939. See H. L. Van Breda, "Maurice Merleau-Ponty et les Archives-Husserl a

Louvain," *Revue de Métaphysique et de morale* 67 (1962): 412. For more details on these articles, but generally on the *economic* question of the transcendental and the evolution of that concept in Merleau-Ponty's writings, see Geraets's classic and amply supported *Vers une nouvelle philosophie transcendantale* (esp. chap. 4).

39. Edmund Husserl, "Grundlegende Untersuchungen zum phänomenologischen Ursprung der Räumlichkeit der Natur [Umsturz der kopernikanischen Lehre]," in *Philosophical Essays in Memory of Edmund Husserl,* ed. Marvin Farber (Cambridge, Mass.: Harvard University Press, 1940), 307–25.

40. That idea resurfaces in *The Visible and the Invisible,* where the horizontal field functions as "the model for every transcendence" (*VI,* 280/231).

41. "The transcending of the world . . . does not lead outside of or away from the world to an origin which is separate from the world (and to which the world is connected only by some relation) as if leading us to some *other* world; the phenomenological transcending of the world, as the disclosure of transcendental subjectivity, is at the same time the *retention* [*Einbehaltung*] *of the world* within the universe of absolute 'being' that has been exposed." Fink, "Phenomenological Philosophy of Edmund Husserl," 99. Merleau-Ponty had already cited this work in "The Nature of Perception" (*PrP,* 21/77).

42. "The solipsist illusion . . . consists in thinking that every surpassing is a surpassing accomplished by oneself" (*VI,* 186/143, trans. modified).

2. Language

1. Cf. regarding Spinoza: "Spinoza would not have spent so much time considering a drowning fly if this behavior had not offered to the eye something other than a fragment of extension; the theory of animal machines is a 'resistance' to the phenomenon of behavior. Therefore this phenomenon must still be conceptualized. The structure of behavior as it presents itself to perceptual experience is neither thing nor consciousness; and it is this which renders it opaque to the mind" (*SC,* 137/127).

2. Merleau-Ponty develops this point in more detail in his nature lectures. Although he rejects any conception of language as the translation of a preexisting thought, he demonstrates the internal contradictions of naturalizing theories: "A very common idea: Cybernetics, the theory of information=a stimulus is a 'message'" (*N,* 289/226). Although cybernetics had taken a decisive step in emancipating the living thing from its biological determinations and considering it as a symbolic being, it had the tendency, by virtue of its origin in classic information theory, to reduce it to a communicating machine. But to conceive the interaction of the living thing on the message/receptor model is to fall back into the old theory of reflexes.

3. See also Renaud Barbaras, "De la parole à l'être: Le problème de l'expression comme voie d'accès à l'ontologie," in *Merleau-Ponty: Le philosophe et son langage,* ed. François Heidsieck (Paris: Centre National de la Recherche Scientifique, 1993), 67.

4. See also Bernhard Waldenfels, "The Paradox of Expression," trans. Chris Nagel, in *Chiasms: Merleau-Ponty's Notion of Flesh*, ed. Fred Evans and Leonard Lawlor (Albany: State University of New York Press, 2000), 89–102.

5. Cf. Alessandro Delcò, *Merleau-Ponty et l'expérience de la création: Du paradigme au schème* (Paris: Presses Universitaires de France, 2005), esp. the chapter "Le problème de l'insertion directe du discursif dans le gestuel," 97–101.

6. The impasses of the "emotivist" explanation have often been pointed out. See esp. Gary Brent Madison, *The Phenomenology of Merleau-Ponty: A Search for the Limits of Consciousness*, trans. Gary Brent Madison (Athens: Ohio University Press, 1981), 127–28; Renaud Barbaras, *Le tournant de l'expérience: Recherches sur la philosophie de Merleau-Ponty* (Paris: Vrin, 1998), 189–91.

7. Merleau-Ponty reminds us that culture conditions the expression of emotional states such as love or anger, taking the examples of Japan and the Trobrianders of Papua New Guinea (*PP*, 220/531nn19, 20). In *Phenomenology of Perception,* as has often been pointed out, there is a permanent tension between an effort to avoid any reductive or naïve theory and an emphasis on the "first word" and "primordial meaning" that supposedly precedes all cultural relativization.

8. That almost structuralist idea of expression anticipates Merleau-Ponty's readings of Saussurean linguists (see the section titled "The Diacritical" in this chapter). In the Sorbonne course titled "Child Psychology and Pedagogy," based primarily on analyses of cases already cited in *Phenomenology of Perception,* the influence of structural linguistics is apparent. That suggests a new way of looking at the aporias that surface in *Phenomenology:* "There are no purely natural expressions, nor are there any purely social or conventional expressions" (*PPE*, 556/447).

9. We still do not have access to many of the manuscripts from these years, since they have not yet been placed in the Merleau-Ponty collection at the Bibliothèque Nationale.

10. H. J. Pos, "Phenomenology and Linguistics" (1939), trans. Robin M. Muller, *Graduate Faculty Philosophy Journal* 31, no. 1 (2010): 35–44. Merleau-Ponty's later text "On the Phenomenology of Language" should no doubt be seen as the muted echo of Pos's article (*SG,* 105–22/84–97).

11. There is now a rich bibliography on the connections between Merleau-Ponty's philosophy and the field of linguistics. See esp. Luce Fontaine-De Visscher, *Phénomène ou structure? Essai sur le langage chez Merleau-Ponty* (Brussels: Facultés Universitaires Saint-Louis, 1974); Regula Giuliani-Tagmann, *Sprache und Erfahrung in der Schriften von Maurice Merleau-Ponty* (Bern: Lang, 1983), esp. 102–11; Yves Thierry, *Du corps parlant: Le langage chez Merleau-Ponty* (Brussels: Ousia, 1987); Stefan Bucher, *Zwischen Phänomenologie und Sprachwissenschaft: Zu Merleau-Pontys Theorie der Sprache* (Münster: Nodus, 1991); Salvatore Constantino, *La testimonianza del linguaggio: Saggio su*

Merleau-Ponty (Milan: Franco Angeli, 1999), esp. 57–94; Daniel Oskui, "Wider den Metaphernzwang: Merleau-Ponty und die sprachliche Produktivität bei Chomsky, Bühler und Ricoeur," in *Merleau-Ponty und die Kulturwissenschaften,* ed. Regula Giuliani (Munich: Fink, 2000), 99–141.

12. Paul Ricoeur, "The Question of the Subject: The Challenge of Semiology," in his *The Conflict of Interpretations,* ed. Don Ihde, trans. Kathleen McLaughlin (Evanston, Ill.: Northwestern University Press, 1974), 247, 250. Remigius C. Kwant had already pronounced a similar judgment in *From Phenomenology to Metaphysics* (Pittsburgh: Duquesne University Press, 1966), esp. 176.

13. Fontaine-De Visscher, *Phénomène ou structure?* 18.

14. Roland Barthes, *Elements of Semiology,* trans. Annette Lavers and Colin Smith (New York: Hill and Wang, 1968), 24.

15. It should be obvious that his rendering of the difference between the synchronic and the diachronic is rather shaky. Merleau-Ponty claims there is a "diachronic linguistics of language" standing in contrast to the "synchronic linguistics of language." In Saussure, however, the distinction between synchrony and diachrony is at work only within language. Is this merely a misreading? Some interpreters have suggested that it could be seen as an implicit but nonetheless coherent distortion, whose aim would be to make up for certain lacunae in Saussure's system. In any event, the proximity between Merleau-Ponty's hypotheses about the diachronic and the correction of Saussure's theories—by heirs of Saussure as different as Trubetzkoy and Gustave Guillaume—using the dimension of time would lead in that direction.

16. Edmund Husserl, *Logical Investigations,* ed. Dermot Moran, trans. J. N. Findlay. 2 vols. Vol. 2: *Investigations in Phenomenology and Knowledge* (London: Routledge, 2001), 73–74.

17. Ibid., 74. Cf. *PM,* 37/25.

18. I am following here the interpretation proposed by Mauro Carbone, "La dicibilité du monde: La période intermédiaire de la pensée de Merleau-Ponty à partir de Saussure," in *Merleau-Ponty: Le philosophe et son langage,* ed. Heidsieck, 83–99.

19. Although this connection is not made by Merleau-Ponty, there is reason to wonder whether there is not, in the belated developments of the notion of "institution" (apart from the obvious inspiration of the Husserlian *Stiftung*), a subliminal return of Saussure.

20. Ferdinand de Saussure, *Course on General Linguistics,* ed. Charles Bally and Albert Séchehaye, trans. Wade Baskin (New York: Philosophical Library, 1959), 68–69. I leave aside the philological problems associated with the *Course* and analyze only Merleau-Ponty's Saussure, that is, the one who emerges from Bally and Séchehaye's retranscriptions.

21. Ibid., 69.

22. Tullio de Mauro's example, cited in his introduction to Ferdinand de Saussure, *Cours de linguistique générale,* ed. Charles Bally and Albert Séchehaye, critical edition by Tullio de Mauro (Paris: Payot, 2005), viii.

23. On this matter, see Giorgio Agamben's writings on the Aristotelian *dynamis,* considered not in terms of actualization but as the possibility of nonaction. The best literary illustration is no doubt Bartleby's "I would prefer not to" in Herman Melville's "Bartleby, the Scrivener," to which Deleuze and Agamben have devoted memorable analyses. See, first, "Bartleby, or, The Formula," Deleuze's preface to the French translation of Herman Melville's *The Encantatas, or Enchanted Isles: Les îles enchantées, Le Campanile,* trans. Michèle Causse (Paris: Flammarion, 1989), in Gilles Deleuze, *Essays Critical and Clinical,* trans. Daniel W. Smith and Michael A. Greco (Minneapolis: University of Minnesota Press, 1997), 68–90; then, Agamben's "Bartleby, or On Contingency," in *Collected Essays in Philosophy,* ed. Daniel Heller-Roazen (Stanford: Stanford University Press, 1999), 243–71.

24. Preparatory note for the course "Recherches sur l'usage littéraire du langage" ("Research on the Literary Use of Language"), taught at the Collège de France, 1952–53. That idea was already outlined in *Phenomenology of Perception,* when, in reaction to the theory of the arbitrariness of the sign, Merleau-Ponty writes that "if we use the word *'nuit'* for night, then it would not be arbitrary that we use *'lumière'* for light" (*PP,* 218/193). In retrospect, this can be seen as an intuition that it is pertinent to define signs as arbitrary only in combination with their differential character, that is, the mutual dependence of signs on one another.

25. Remark in the reading notes on Paul Valéry.

26. That interpretation is actually very superficial, since we need only refer to the section in the *Course on General Linguistics* titled "Absolute and Relative Arbitrariness" to realize that a partly motivated arbitrariness is perfectly well envisioned (131–34).

27. It is noteworthy that the exact turn of phrase "prose of the world" is used not in Hegel's theory of history but rather in his *Aesthetics:* "This is the prose of the world, as it appears to the consciousness of the individual himself and of others:—a world of finitude and mutability, of entanglement in the relative, of the pressure of necessity from which the individual is in no position to withdraw." G. W. F. Hegel, *Aesthetics: Lectures on Fine Art,* trans. T. M. Knox, 2 vols. (Oxford: Clarendon, 1975), 1:150.

28. Jean-Paul Sartre, *What Is Literature?* trans. Bernard Frechtman (New York: Philosophical Library, n.d. [1949]), 12, 19, trans. slightly modified.

29. Ibid., 20, trans. modified.

30. Ibid.

31. Ibid., 25, trans. modified.

32. Ibid., 18, 21, 25.

33. Saussure, *Course,* 22–23.

34. Ibid.

35. Husserl, *Logical Investigations,* 1:210. In the original: "Die Schachfiguren kommen im Spiel nicht als diese so und so geformten und gefärbten Dinge aus Elfenbein, Holz u. dgl. in Betracht. Was sie phänomenal und

physisch konstituiert, ist ganz gleichgültig und kann nach Willkür wechseln. Zu Schachfiguren, d.i. zu Spielmarken des fraglichen Spiels, werden sie vielmehr durch die Spielregeln, welche ihnen ihre feste *Spielbedeutung* geben" (*Hua* 19.1:74).

36. On several occasions Merleau-Ponty quoted this passage from *Formale und transzendentale Logik:* "Redend vollziehen wir fortlaufend ein inneres, sich mit den Worten verschmelzendes, sich gleichsam beseelendes Meinen. Der Erfolg dieser Beseelung ist, dass die Worte und die ganzen Reden in sich eine Meinung gleichsam *verleiblichen* und verleiblicht in sich als Sinn tragen" (*Hua* 17:26–27). Note as well that the expression *Sprachleib* appears in the unpublished text Merleau-Ponty studied during his stay in Leuven in 1939, published in Jacques Derrida, *Edmund Husserl's Origin of Geometry: An Introduction,* trans. John P. Leavey (Lincoln: University of Nebraska Press, 1989), 161. On the role of *Leib* in Husserl, see Didier Franck, *Flesh and Body: On the Phenomenology of Husserl,* trans. Joseph Rivera and Scott Davidson (London: Bloomsbury, 2014). For the question of corporeality in Heidegger, about which Sartre is said to have remarked that *Sein und Zeit* (*Being and Time*) does not dedicate even six lines to it, one must rather turn to the Zollikon seminars of the later Heidegger. On this matter, see Jocelyn Benoist, "Chair et corps dans les séminaires de Zollikon: La différence et le reste," in *Autour de Husserl: L'ego et la raison* (Paris: Vrin, 1994), 107–22.

37. For a fuller presentation of this argument, see my "The Diacritical Nature of Meaning: Merleau-Ponty with Saussure," *Chiasmi International: Trilingual Studies concerning Merleau-Ponty's Thought* 15 (2013): 167–80.

38. Correlatively, it may be pointed that, in a working note of October 27, 1959, perception is called a "diacritical, relative, oppositional system" (*VI*, 262/213).

39. Edmund Husserl, *Cartesian Meditations,* trans. Dorion Cairns (The Hague: Nijhoff, 1973), §19, pp. 44–45.

40. For the history and transformations of that "little phrase," see Jacques Taminiaux, *Le regard et l'excédent* (The Hague: Nijhoff, 1977), chap. 6, "Expérience, l'expression et la forme dans l'itinéraire de Merleau-Ponty," 90–115.

41. See my "La parole oblique: Merleau-Ponty et les enjeux d'une éthique de l'indirect," *Phainomenon: Revista de Fenomenologia* 18 (2011): 157–74.

42. Several studies have recently highlighted the role, often marginalized by early commentators, of music as a fertile source of the later Merleau-Ponty's thought. Although these studies have the merit of presenting a more balanced portrait of the author, no one has called into doubt the fact that the visual arts—along with literature—remained Merleau-Ponty's essential inspiration. In November 1959, Merleau-Ponty attended a performance of Beethoven's *Leonore,* no. 2, the first version of the overture to *Fidelio,* which prompted him to compare music to painting. Insofar as each of them is in its own way an art of silence, they converge toward philosophy: "Music, like painting, is to the sensible world what philosophy is to the world as a whole" (MBN 8.2, fol. 289),

unpublished note of November 15, 1959. On the role of music, see also Lambert Dousson's cogent article "L'ambiguïté sans système: La musique dans la philosophie de Merleau-Ponty," in *Du sensible à l'oeuvre: Esthétiques de Merleau-Ponty*, ed. Emmanuel Alloa and Adnen Jdey (Brussels: La Lettre volée, 2012), 209–32.

3. Ontology of the Visible

1. I cannot resist pointing out the parallels with Levinas, who is known to have completely changed his language following Derrida's critique in "Violence and Metaphysics," which reproached him for the incommensurability between the aspiration to establish metaphysics on new foundations and his continued use, in *Totality and Infinity*, of the traditional vocabulary he sought to move beyond.

2. Mikel Dufrenne, "Maurice Merleau-Ponty" (1962), in his *Jalons* (The Hague: Nijhoff, 1966), 208–21, esp. 215.

3. This is Emmanuel Levinas's verdict in his preface to Theodore Geraets, *Vers une nouvelle philosophie transcendantale: La genèse de la philosophie de Maurice Merleau-Ponty jusqu'à la Phénoménologie de la Perception*, with a preface by Emmanuel Levinas (The Hague: Nijhoff, 1971), ix. Merleau-Ponty himself moves in that direction, especially in his remarks at the 1961 colloquium "Sens et usages du terme structure dans les sciences humaines et sociales," January 11, 1961.

4. On the hole in Hegel, cf. *PP*, 249/223. See also *VI*, 249/196: "The open, in the sense of a *hole,* that is Sartre, is Bergson, is negativism or ultra positivism (Bergson)—indiscernible."

5. Cf. "Vision is no longer a gaze on an 'outside,' representation" (*NC*, 170).

6. Cf. Claude Lefort's indications in the preface to *OE* (vi).

7. As early as "Cézanne's Doubt," Merleau-Ponty writes that "words do not look like the things they designate; and so a picture is not a trompe-l'oeil" (*SNS*, 23/17, trans. modified).

8. André Malraux, *Les voix du silence* (Paris, NRF, 1951). [*The Voices of Silence : Man and His Art*, trans. Stuart Gilbert (New York: Doubleday, 1953).]

9. André Malraux, *Psychologie de l'art*, vol. 2: *La creation artistique* (Geneva: Skira, 1949). [*Psychology of Art*, vol. 2: *The Creative Act*, trans. Stuart Gilbert. (London: Zwemmer, 1949).]

10. Edmund Husserl, *Ideas Pertaining to a Pure Phenomenology and to a Phenomenological Philosophy,* book 2: *Studies in the Phenomenology of Constitution,* trans. Richard Rojcewicz and André Schuwer (Dordrecht: Kluwer, 1989), §61, p. 290 (*Hua* 4:277).

11. Edmund Husserl, *The Crisis of European Sciences and Transcendental Phenomenology*, trans. David Carr. Evanston, Ill.: Northwestern University Press, 1970, 31 (orig, *Hua* 6:28).

12. Ibid., 30.

13. Ibid., 31.

14. Éliane Escoubas, adopting Maurice Blanchot's expression, has shown that it is possible to speak of a Merleau-Pontian "aesthetics without works" or

an aesthetics of "being out of work" (*désoeuvrement*): Éliane Escoubas, "La question de l'oeuvre d'art: Merleau-Ponty et Heidegger," in *Merleau-Ponty: Phénoménologie et expériences*, ed. Marc Richir and Étienne Tassin (Grenoble: Millon, 1992), 123–38. Indeed, Merleau-Ponty never provides philosophical analyses of *single* works of arts: The individual work is conspicuously absent, despite—or rather *because of*—his proximity to the creative process of the artists themselves. See my own developments on this point in "Du sensible à l'oeuvre : Sur le rapport entre Merleau-Ponty et les arts," in *Du sensible à l'oeuvre: Esthétiques de Merleau-Ponty*, ed. Emmanuel Alloa and Adnen Jdey (Brussels: La Lettre volée, 2012), 16–18.

15. In a working note of February 1959, Merleau-Ponty writes: "Results of *Ph.P.* [*Phenomenology of Perception*]—*Necessity* of bringing them to ontological explicitation" (*VI*, 234/183). This ontological turn, however, can be traced back to writings from the early 1950s. In "Everywhere and Nowhere," Merleau-Ponty writes that a concrete philosophy would have to "stick close to experience, and yet not limit itself to the empirical but restore to each experience the ontological cipher which marks it internally" (*SG*, 155/157). On this ontological turn, see Renaud Barbaras, *The Being of the Phenomenon: Merleau-Ponty's Ontology,* trans. Ted Toadvine and Leonard Lawlor (Bloomington: Indiana University Press, 2004), as well as Emmanuel de Saint-Aubert, *Vers une ontologie indirecte: Sources et enjeux critiques de l'appel à l'ontologie chez Merleau-Ponty* (Paris: Vrin, 2006).

16. Aristotle, *Historia animalium* 490a1–3.

17. How can we not hear the Christological connotations here? Gilles Deleuze will take the opposing view, speaking, with respect to Bacon's paintings, of an aesthetics of "meat." But does that depart from the register of Christian representation, which rests, precisely, on the display of dead flesh? There is reason to doubt it. For a more general contextualization of the notion of flesh and the many misunderstandings surrounding it in contemporary philosophy, see Mauro Carbone, "Flesh: Towards the History of a Misunderstanding," in his *The Flesh of Images: Merleau-Ponty between Painting and Cinema*, trans. Marta Nijhuis (Albany: State University of New York Press, 2015), 7–20.

18. Geraets, *Vers une nouvelle philosophie transcendantale*, 181.

19. Emmanuel de Saint-Aubert, *Du lien des êtres aux éléments de l'être: Merleau-Ponty au tournant des années 1945–1951* (Paris: Vrin, 2004), 158.

20. This is itself a classic topos: Husserl represented merely a late stage in its history, which runs from Theophrastus to Condillac.

21. See Jacques Derrida, *Voice and Phenomenon: Introduction to the Problem of the Sign in Husserl's Phenomenology,* trans. Leonard Lawlor (Evanston, Ill.: Northwestern University Press, 2011).

22. Nevertheless, Derrida devoted one of his classes to *The Visible and the Invisible* when it was first published (Sorbonne class of May 15, 1964, Derrida Archive, University of California Irvine).

23. Emmanuel Levinas, *Totality and Infinity: An Essay on Exteriority*, trans. Alphonso Lingis (Dordrecht: Kluwer, 1991), 35.

24. That formulation is reminiscent of Husserl's own solution, which—as Bernhard Waldenfels has often noted—describes the foreign in terms of an "accessibility of what is originally inaccessible" (*Zugänglichkeit des original Unzugänglichen*) (*Hua* 1:144).

25. The expression "palpating with the gaze" dates back to *Phenomenology of Perception* (e.g., *PP*, 243/218, trans. modified) and continues through to *The Visible and the Invisible* (*VI*, 175/131, trans. modified). The continuity between touch and vision is also motivated: "The very fact that genuine vision is prepared for through a transition phase and through a sort of touching with the eyes could not be understood if there were no quasi-spatial tactile fields into which the first visual perceptions could be inserted" (*PP*, 258/232).

26. Jacques Derrida, "Tangent III," in *On Touching: Jean-Luc Nancy*, trans. Christine Irizarry (Stanford: Stanford University Press, 2005), 213.

27. So argues Claude Lefort in "Qu'est-ce que voir?" in *Sur une colonne absente: Écrits autour de Merleau-Ponty* (Paris: Gallimard, 1978), 140–55, esp. 140.

28. For Heraclitus, the eyes are the most astute witnesses (ἀκριέστεροι μάρτυρες) (Diels-Kranz frag. 22, B 101). The same trope recurs in Plato (*Phaedrus* 250d).

29. See the famous beginning of the *Metaphysics:* "We prefer sight, generally speaking, to all the other senses" (*Metaphysics* A.1.980a21, Loeb Classical Library).

30. On this alleged general "denigration of touch," see my attempts at a more balanced account of touch in Western, post-Aristotelian metaphysics: "Getting in Touch: Aristotelian Diagnostics," in *Carnal Hermeneutics*, ed. Richard Kearney and Brian Treanor (New York: Fordham University Press, 2015), 195–213.

31. Husserl, *Ideas Pertaining to a Pure Phenomenology*, book 2, §36, p. 152.

32. Husserl, *Cartesian Meditations*, §44, p. 97, trans. modified.

33. Husserl, *Ideas*, book 2, §37, p. 158.

34. Ibid., 155n1.

35. This position is much more common that one might think. Martin Jay reminds us that, since Simplicius's commentary *De anima*, an entire current of thought continuing into the eighteenth century considered touch the master sense, at the expense of vision (Martin Jay, *Downcast Eyes: The Denigration of Vision in Twentieth-Century French Thought* [Berkeley: University of California Press, 1993], esp. 34–35).

36. Husserl, *Ideas*, §37, p. 155.

37. I borrow this expression from Françoise Dastur's luminous article "World, Flesh, Vision," trans. Ted Toadvine, in *Chiasms: Merleau-Ponty's Notion of Flesh*, ed. Fred Evans and Leonard Lawlor (Albany: State University of New York Press, 2000), 39.

38. Ibid., 97. Derrida also returns to these expressions in *On Touching,* 200–1.

39. This title already appears in "The Metaphysical in Man" (*SNS,* 115/94n13).

40. These reflections echo a set of unpublished and undated texts from late 1958 titled "The Complex of Western Ontology, or, The Cartesian Ontological Complex" (MBN 6, fol. 67–95).

41. Despite the reservations Merleau-Ponty expresses here, the importance played by Martial Guéroult's *Descartes selon l'ordre de raison* (vol. 1: *L'Âme et Dieu,* and vol. *2: L'Âme et le corps* (Paris: Aubier-Montaigne, 1953) [*Descartes' Philosophy Interpreted according to the Order of Reasons,* vol. 1: *The Soul and God,* and vol. 2: *The Soul and the Body,* trans. Roger Ariew (Minneapolis: University of Minnesota Press, 1984–85)]) in the reactivation of his reading of Descartes is well known. The study Guéroult dedicated and sent to the new faculty member of the Collège de France in June 1953 became the object of an in-depth study beginning in 1956, as attested by many marginal notes. See Emmanuel de Saint-Aubert, *Le scénario cartésien: Recherches sur la formation et la cohérence de l'intention philosophique de Merleau-Ponty* (Paris: Vrin, 2005). An admiring nod in passing to Saint-Aubert's Herculean task: in three volumes, he revisits Merleau-Ponty's oeuvre in the light all the unpublished texts, an approach more necessary now than ever before, to counter the reductionism of all sorts of which its author is very often the victim.

42. See the working notes found on his desk on May 3, 1961 (MBN 19, fol. 54–87).

43. The expression was devised in 1947 by the Cartesian philosopher François Alquié in his "Une philosophie de l'ambiguïté: L'existentialisme de Maurice Merleau-Ponty" (*Fontaine* 9, no. 59 [1947]: 47–70) and was adopted by Alphonse Waelhens in *Une philosophie de l'ambiguïté: L'existentialisme de Maurice Merleau-Ponty* (1951; Leuven: Publications Universitaires, 1978).

44. Clearly, Merleau-Ponty was again inspired by Valéry, who, in a 1924 note appearing in his *Cahiers (Notebooks),* describes Frans Hals's portrait of Descartes (1649, Paris, Louvre). The right eyebrow is raised, a detail generally interpreted as a sign of doubt. Valéry, by contrast, sees it as an "unsteadiness" betraying "double vision" (Paul Valéry, *Cahiers* [Paris: Gallimard, 1973], 1:598). See Bernhard Waldenfels, *Idiome des Denkens: Deutsch-Französische Gedankengänge II* (Frankfurt: Suhrkamp, 2005), 14.

45. Ancient Greek had no word for "sensation" in the strict sense.

46. René Descartes, "Optics," in *Discourse on Method, Optics, Geometry, and Meteorology,* trans. Paul J. Olscamp, rev. ed. (Indianapolis: Hackett, 2001), 67.

47. Ibid., 70.

48. "I observed that nothing at all belonged to the nature or essence of body, except that it was a thing with length, breadth, and depth, admitting of various shapes and various motions." René Descartes, "Reply to Objections VI," §10, in *The Philosophical Works of Descartes,* trans. Elizabeth S. Haldane and G. R. T. Ross, 2 vols. (Cambridge: University of Cambridge Press, 1970), 2:253–54.

49. "Colours, odours, savours, and the rest of such things . . . were merely sensations existing in my thought, and differing no less from bodies than pain differs from the shape and motion of the instrument which inflicts it" (ibid., 254).

50. See the chapter "L'aisthêsis comme l'impensé de Descartes," in *L'expression au-delà de la représentation: Sur l'aisthêsis et l'esthétique chez Merleau-Ponty*, by Jenny Slatman (Leuven: Peeters, 2001), 86–91. For a comparison of Descartes's position to other theories of vision, see—despite its shortcomings—Aurora Plomer's *Phenomenology, Geometry and Vision: Merleau-Ponty's Critique of Classical Theories of Vision* (Aldershot, U.K.: Gower, 1991).

51. In *The Prose of the World*, Merleau-Ponty writes that "in language, truth is not an adequation but anticipation, repetition, and slippage of meaning. Truth allows itself to be reached only through a sort of distance" (*PM*, 180–81/129). His interest in language may have already been motivated by the fact that it represents a kind of "action at a distance" (*SG* 144/89).

52. Henri Bergson, *Creative Evolution*, trans. Arthur Mitchell (New York: Modern Library, 1944), 300–24. For a comparison between the critique of Bergsonian nothingness and the question of phenomenological reduction, see Renaud Barbaras, *Desire and Distance: Introduction to a Phenomenology of Perception* (Stanford: Stanford University Press, 2006), "Phenomenological Reduction as a Critique of Nothingness," 44–61.

53. Maurice Blondel, *L'être et les êtres* (Paris: Alcan, 1935).

54. Ibid., 368.

Conclusion: Toward Dia-Phenomenology

1. Michel de Certeau, "The Madness of Vision," trans. Michael B. Smith, *Enclitic* 7, no. 1 (1983): 24.

2. Edmund Husserl, *The Crisis of European Sciences and Transcendental Phenomenology*, trans. David Carr (Evanston, Ill.: Northwestern University Press, 1970), 295 (*Hua* 6:343), trans. modified.

3. The idea of an encroachment of things actually originated in the optical phenomenon of overlapping, highlighted by Max Wertheimer's Gestaltist school. Here Merleau-Ponty gives the notion a new, ontological meaning.

4. Jean-Paul Sartre, *Being and Nothingness: An Essay on Phenomenological Ontology*, translated with an introduction by Hazel E. Barnes (New York: Philosophical Library, 1956), pt. 3, chap. 1, sec. 4.

5. For a detailed reconstruction of the theory of the medium in Aristotle and the troubled history of its reception up to the modern period, I take the liberty of referring the reader to my *Das durchscheinende Bild: Konturen einer medialen Phänomenologie* (Berlin: diaphanes, 2011).

6. Aristotle, *On the Soul*, trans. W. S. Hett (Cambridge, Mass.: Harvard University Press, 1957), II 7, 419a20–21.

7. Ibid., II 7, 419b22.

8. Ibid., II 11, 423b8.

Selected Bibliography

For works by Maurice Merleau-Ponty see the list of abbreviations at the beginning of the book.

On Merleau-Ponty

Alloa, Emmanuel. "The Diacritical Nature of Meaning: Merleau-Ponty with Saussure." *Chiasmi International: Trilingual Studies Concerning Merleau-Ponty's Thought* 15 (2013): 167–80.

———. "La parole oblique: Merleau-Ponty et les enjeux d'une éthique de l'indirect." *Phainomenon: Revista de Fenomenologia* 18 (2011): 157–74.

———. "Merleau-Ponty II: Fleisch und Differenz." In *Leiblichkeit: Geschichte und Aktualität eines Konzepts,* edited by E. Alloa, T. Bedorf, C. Grüny, and T. Klass, 37–51. Tübingen: Mohr Siebeck, 2012.

———. "The Theatre of the Virtual: How to Stage Potentialities with Merleau-Ponty." In *Encounters in Performance Philosophy*, edited by Laura Cull and Alice Lagaay, 147–70. Basingstoke: Palgrave Macmillan, 2014.

Alloa, Emmanuel, and Adnen Jdey, eds. *Du sensible à l'oeuvre: Esthétiques de Merleau-Ponty.* Brussels: La Lettre volée, 2012.

Alquié, François. "Une philosophie de l'ambiguïté: L'existentialisme de Maurice Merleau-Ponty." *Fontaine* 11, no. 59 (1947): 47–70.

Barbaras, Renaud. "De la parole à l'être: Le problème de l'expression comme voie d'accès à l'ontologie." In *Merleau-Ponty: Le philosophe et son langage,* edited by François Heidsieck, 61–82. Paris: Centre National de la Recherche Scientifique. 1993.

———. *De l'être du phénomène: Sur l'ontologie de Merleau-Ponty.* Grenoble: Million, 1990. [*The Being of the Phenomenon: Merleau-Ponty's Ontology.*

Translated by Ted Toadvine and Leonard Lawlor. Bloomington: Indiana University Press, 2004.]

———. "La réduction phénoménologique comme critique du néant." In his *Le désir et la distance: Introduction à une phénoménologie de la perception*. Paris: Vrin, 1999. ["Phenomenological Reduction as a Critique of Nothingness." In *Desire and Distance: Introduction to a Phenomenology of Perception*, 44–61. Stanford: Stanford University Press, 2006.]

———. *Le tournant de l'expérience: Recherches sur la philosophie de Merleau-Ponty*. Paris: Vrin, 1998.

———. "Perception et pulsion." *Alter: Revue de phénoménologie* 9 (2001): 13–26. Repr. in his *Vie et intentionnalité—Recherches phénoménologiques*. Paris: Vrin, 2003.

Bermes, Christian. "Medialität—Anthropologisches Radikal oder ontologisches Prinzip? Merleau-Pontys Ausführung der Phänomenologie." In *Die Stellung des Menschen in der Kultur: Festschrift für Ernst Wolfgang Orth zum 65. Geburtstag*, edited by Christian Bermes, Julia Jonas, and Karl-Heinz Lembeck, 41–58. Würzburg: Königshausen & Neumann, 2002.

Bimbenet, Étienne. *Nature et humanité: Le problème anthropologique dans l'oeuvre de Merleau-Ponty*. Paris: Vrin, 2004.

Bucher, Stefan. *Zwischen Phänomenologie und Sprachwissenschaft: Zu Merleau-Pontys Theorie der Sprache*. Münster: Nodus, 1991.

Carbone, Mauro. "Alla ricerca dell'a-filosofia: Merleau-Ponty e la *Einleitung* alla *Phänomenologie des Geistes*." In *Negli specchi dell'essere: Saggi sulla filosofia di Merleau-Ponty*, edited by Mauro Carbone and Claudio Fontana, 211–35. Milan: Hestia, 1993. ["*Ad Limina Philosophiae*: Merleau-Ponty and the 'Introduction' to Hegel's *Phenomenology of Spirit*." Translated by Nicoletta Grillo and David Michael Levin. In Mauro Carbone, *The Thinking of the Sensible: Merleau-Ponty's A-Philosophy*, 14–27. Evanston, Ill.: Northwestern University Press, 2004.]

———. "La dicibilité du monde: La période intermédiaire de la pensée de Merleau-Ponty à partir de Saussure." In *Merleau-Ponty: Le philosophe et son langage*, edited by François Heidsieck, 83–99. Paris: Centre National de la Recherche Scientifique, 1993.

———. *La visibilité de l'invisible: Merleau-Ponty entre Cézanne et Proust*. Hildesheim: Olms, 2001.

———. "Flesh: Towards the History of a Misunderstanding." In his *The Flesh of Images: Merleau-Ponty between Painting and Cinema*, translated by Marta Nijhuis, 7–20. Albany: State University of New York Press, 2015.

Certeau, Michel de. "La folie de la vision." *Esprit* 66 (1982): 89–99. ["The Madness of Vision." Translated by Michael B. Smith. *Enclitic* 7, no. 1 (1983): 24–31.]

Chadarevian, Soraya de. *Zwischen den Diskursen: Merleau-Ponty und die Wissenschaften*. Würzburg: Königshausen & Neumann, 1990.

Costantino, Salvatore. *La testimonianza del linguaggio: Saggio su Merleau-Ponty.* Milan: FrancoAngeli, 1999.

Dastur, Françoise. "Merleau-Ponty et la pensée du dedans." In *Merleau-Ponty: Phénoménologie et expériences,* edited by Marc Richir and Étienne Tassin, 42–65. Grenoble: Millon, 1992. ["Merleau-Ponty and Thinking from Within." In *Merleau-Ponty in Contemporary Perspective,* edited by Patrick Burke and Jan van Der Veken, 25–35. Dordrecht: Kluwer, 1993.]

———. "Monde, Chair, Vision." In her *Chair et langage: Essais sur Merleau-Ponty,* 69–107. Versanne: Encre Marine, 2001. ["World, Flesh, Vision." Translated by Ted Toadvine. In *Chiasms: Merleau-Ponty's Notion of Flesh,* edited by Fred Evans and Leonard Lawlor, 23–49. Albany: State University of New York Press, 2000.]

Delcò, Alessandro. *Merleau-Ponty et l'expérience de la création: Du paradigme au schème.* Paris: Presses Universitaires de France, 2005.

Derrida, Jacques. "Tangente III." In his *Jean-Luc Nancy: Le toucher.* Paris: Galilée, 2000. ["Tangent III." In his *On Touching: Jean-Luc Nancy.* Translated by Christine Irizarry. Stanford: Stanford University Press, 2005.]

Dufrenne, Mikel. "Maurice Merleau-Ponty." In *Jalons,* 208–21. The Hague: Nijhoff, 1966.

Escoubas, Éliane. "La question de l'oeuvre d'art: Merleau-Ponty et Heidegger." In *Merleau-Ponty: Phénoménologie et expériences.* Edited by Marc Richir and Étienne Tassin, 123–38. Grenoble: Millon, 1992.

Fontaine-De Visscher, Luce. *Phénomène ou structure? Essai sur le langage chez Merleau-Ponty.* Brussels: Facultés Universitaires Saint-Louis, 1974.

Geraets, Theodore F. *Vers une nouvelle philosophie transcendantale: La genèse de la philosophie de Maurice Merleau-Ponty jusqu'à la Phénoménologie de la Perception.* With a preface by Emmanuel Levinas. The Hague: Nijhoff, 1971.

Giuliani-Tagmann, Regula. *Sprache und Erfahrung in den Schriften von Maurice Merleau-Ponty.* Bern: Peter Lang, 1983.

Kwant, Remigius C. *From Phenomenology to Metaphysics.* Pittsburgh, Pa.: Duquesne University Press, 1966.

Lefort, Claude. "Qu'est-ce que voir?" In his *Sur une colonne absente: Écrits autour de Merleau-Ponty,* 140–55. Paris: Gallimard, 1978.

Madison, Gary Brent. *La phénoménologie de Merleau-Ponty: Une recherche des limites de la conscience.* Paris: Klincksieck, 1973. [*The Phenomenology of Merleau-Ponty: A Search for the Limits of Consciousness.* Translated by Gary Brent Madison. Athens: Ohio University Press, 1981.]

Oskui, Daniel. "Wider den Metaphernzwang: Merleau-Ponty und die sprachliche Produktivität bei Chomsky, Bühler und Ricoeur." In *Merleau-Ponty und die Kulturwissenschaften,* edited by Regula Giuliani, 99–141. Munich: Fink, 2000.

Plomer, Aurora. *Phenomenology, Geometry and Vision: Merleau-Ponty's Critique of Classical Theories of Vision.* Aldershot, U.K.: Gower, 1991.

Saint-Aubert, Emmanuel de. *Du lien des êtres aux éléments de l'être: Merleau-Ponty au tournant des années 1945–1951.* Paris: Vrin, 2004.

―――. *Le scénario cartésien: Recherches sur la formation et la cohérence de l'intention philosophique de Merleau-Ponty.* Paris: Vrin, 2005.

―――. *Vers une ontologie indirecte: Sources et enjeux critiques de l'appel à l'ontologie chez Merleau-Ponty.* Paris: Vrin, 2006.

Slatman, Jenny. *L'expression au-delà de la représentation: Sur l'aisthêsis et l'esthétique chez Merleau-Ponty.* Leuven: Peeters, 2001.

Thierry, Yves. *Du corps parlant: Le langage chez Merleau-Ponty.* Brussels: Ousia, 1987.

Vitali Rosati, Marcello. *Corps et virtuel: Itinéraires à partir de Merleau-Ponty.* Paris: L'Harmattan, 2009.

Waelhens, Alphonse de. *Une philosophie de l'ambiguïté: L'existentialisme de Maurice Merleau-Ponty.* 1951. Leuven: Publications Universitaires, 1978.

Waldenfels, Bernhard. *Idiome des Denkens: Deutsch-Französische Gedankengänge II.* Frankfurt: Suhrkamp, 2005.

―――. "The Paradox of Expression." In *Chiasms: Merleau-Ponty's Notion of Flesh,* edited by Fred Evans and Leonard Lawlor, 89–102. Albany: State University of New York Press, 2000.

―――. *Phänomenologie in Frankreich.* Frankfurt: Suhrkamp, 1983.

―――. "Vérité à faire: Merleau-Ponty's Question concerning Truth." *Philosophy Today* 35, no. 2 (1991): 185–94.

Other Works

Agamben, Giorgio. "La formula della creazione." In Giorgio Agamben and Gilles Deleuze, *Bartleby, la formula della creazione.* Macerata: Quodlibet, 1993. ["Bartleby, or On Contingency." In *Potentialities: Collected Essays in Philosophy,* edited by Daniel Heller-Roazen, 243–71. Stanford: Stanford University Press, 1999.]

Alloa, Emmanuel. *Das durchscheinende Bild: Konturen einer medialen Phänomenologie.* Berlin: Diaphanes, 2011.

―――. "Getting in Touch: Aristotelian Diagnostics." In *Carnal Hermeneutics,* edited by Richard Kearney and Brian Treanor, 195–213. New York: Fordham University Press, 2015.

―――. "Suspension et gravité: L'imaginaire sartrien face au Tintoret." *Alter: Revue de phénoménologie* 15 (2007): 123–41.

Aristotle. *On the Soul.* Translated by W. S. Hett. Cambridge, Mass.: Harvard University Press, 1957.

Bachelard, Gaston. *La terre et les rêveries de la volonté: Essai sur l'imagination de la matière.* Paris: Corti, 1947. [*Earth and Reveries of Will: An Essay on the Imagination of Matter.* Translated by Kenneth Haltman. Dallas: Dallas Institute Press, 2002.]

Barthes, Roland. "Éléments de sémiologie." *Communications* 4, no. 1 (1964): 91–135. Repr. in his *L'aventure sémiologique.* Paris: Seuil, 1985. [*Elements of*

Semiology. Translated by Annette Lavers and Colin Smith. New York: Hill and Wang, 1968.]

Benoist, Jocelyn. "Chair et corps dans les séminaires de Zollikon: La différence et le reste." In his *Autour de Husserl: L'ego et la raison,* 107–22. Paris: Vrin, 1994.

Bergson, Henri. *L'évolution créatrice.* Paris: Presses Universitaires de France, 1948. [*Creative Evolution.* Translated by Arthur Mitchell. New York: Modern Library, 1944.]

Blondel, Maurice. *L'être et les êtres.* Paris: Alcan, 1935.

Brunschvicg, Léon. *Les étapes de la philosophie mathématique.* Paris: Alcan, 1912.

Canguilhem, Georges. *La connaissance de la vie.* 1956. 2nd augmented ed. Paris: Vrin, 1992. [*Knowledge of Life.* Translated by Stefanos Geroulanos and Daniela Ginsburg. New York: Fordham University Press, 2008.]

Comte, Auguste. *Philosophie première: Cours de philosophie positive, Leçons 1 à 45.* Edited with notes by Michel Serres, François Dagognet, and Allal Sinaceur. Paris: Hermann, 1975.

Dastur, Françoise. "Pour une zoologie privative." *Alter: Revue de phénoménologie* 3 (1995): 281–317.

Deleuze, Gilles. "Bartleby, ou la formule." Preface to Herman Melville, *Bartleby, Les Iles enchantées, Le Campanile.* Translated by Michèle Causse. Paris: Flammarion, 1989. Repr. in Gilles Deleuze, *Critique et clinique.* Paris: Minuit, 1993. ["Bartleby, or, The Formula." In *Essays Critical and Clinical,* translated by Daniel W. Smith and Michael A. Greco, 68–90. Minneapolis: University of Minnesota Press, 1997.]

Derrida, Jacques. *La voix et le phénomène.* Paris: Presses Universitaires de France, 1967. [*Voice and Phenomenon: Introduction to the Problem of the Sign in Husserl's Phenomenology.* Translated by Leonard Lawlor. Evanston, Ill.: Northwestern University Press, 2011.]

———, trans. *L'origine de la géométrie,* by Edmund Husserl. Paris: Presses Universitaires de France, 1962. [*Edmund Husserl's Origin of Geometry: An Introduction,* by Jacques Derrida. Translated by John P. Leavey. Lincoln: University of Nebraska Press, 1989.]

Descartes, René. *Dioptrique.* In *Oeuvres,* edited by Charles Adam et Paul Tannery. Vol. 6. Paris: Vrin, 1973. ["Optics." In his *Discourse on Method, Optics, Geometry, and Meteorology.* Translated by Paul J. Olscamp. Rev. ed. Indianapolis: Hackett, 2001.]

———. *Réponses aux sixièmes objections.* In *Oeuvres,* edited by Charles Adam and Paul Tannery. Vol. 9, pt. 1. Paris: Vrin, 1973. ["Reply to Objections VI." In *The Philosophical Works of Descartes.* Translated by Elizabeth S. Haldane and G. R. T. Ross. Vol. 2. Cambridge: University of Cambridge Press, 1970.]

Dufrenne, Mikel. *La notion de l'a priori.* Paris: PUF, 1959.

———. *L'inventaire des apriori.* Paris: Bourgois, 1981.

Fink, Eugen. "Die phänomenologische Philosophie Husserls in der gegenwärtigen Kritik." *Kant-Studien* 8, nos. 1–2 (1933): 319–83. Repr. in *Studien zur Phänomenologie (1930–1939)*, 79–156. The Hague: Nijhoff, 1966. ["The Phenomenological Philosophy of Edmund Husserl and Contemporary Criticism," in *The Phenomenology of Edmund Husserl: Selected Critical Readings*, edited by R. O. Elveton, 70–139. Chicago: Quadrangle, 1970.]

Franck, Didier. *Chair et corps: Sur la phénoménologie de Husserl.* Paris: Minuit, 1981. [*Flesh and Body: On the Phenomenology of Husserl.* Translated by Joseph Rivera and Scott Davidson. London: Bloomsbury, 2014.]

Goldstein, Kurt. *Der Aufbau des Organismus: Einführung in die Biologie unter besonderer Berücksichtigung der Erfahrungen am kranken Menschen.* The Hague: Nijhoff, 1934. [*The Organism: A Holistic Approach to Biology Derived from Pathological Data in Man.* New York: American Book Company, 1939.]

Guéroult, Martial. *Descartes selon l'ordre de raison. Volume 1: L'Âme et Dieu & Volume 2: L'Âme et le corps.* Paris: Aubier-Montaigne, 1953 [*Descartes' Philosophy Interpreted according to the Order of Reasons*, vol. 1: *The Soul and God*, and vol. 2: *The Soul and the Body.* Translated by Roger Ariew. Minneapolis: University of Minnesota Press, 1984–1985.]

Handke, Peter. *Versuch über die Müdigkeit.* Frankfurt: Suhrkamp, 1988. ["Essay on Tiredness." In *The Jukebox and Other Essays on Storytelling.* Translated by Ralph Manheim and Krishna Winston. New York: Farrar, Straus and Giroux, 1997.]

Hegel, G. W. F. *Ästhetik.* 1842. Frankfurt: Europäische Verlagsanstalt, 1966. [*Aesthetics: Lectures on Fine Art.* Translated by T. M. Knox. 2 vols. Oxford: Clarendon, 1975.]

Heidegger, Martin. *Becoming Heidegger: On the Trail of His Early Occasional Writings 1910–1927,* edited by Theodore Kisiel and Thomas Sheehan. Evanston, Ill.: Northwestern University Press, 2007.

———. *Die Grundbegriffe der Metaphysik: Welt-Endlichkeit-Einsamkeit.* Frankfurt: Klostermann, 1983. [*The Fundamental Concepts of Metaphysics: World, Finitude, Solitude.* Translated by William McNeill and Nicholas Walker. Bloomington: Indiana University Press, 1995.]

Husserl, Edmund. *Cartesian Meditations: An Introduction to Phenomenology.* Translated by Dorion Cairns. The Hague: Nijhoff, 1973.

———. *The Crisis of European Sciences and Transcendental Phenomenology.* Translated by David Carr. Evanston, Ill.: Northwestern University Press, 1970.

———. "Grundlegende Untersuchungen zum phänomenologischen Ursprung der Räumlichkeit der Natur [Umsturz der kopernikanischen Lehre]." In *Philosophical Essays in Memory of Edmund Husserl,* edited by Marvin Farber, 307–25. Cambridge, Mass.: Harvard University Press, 1940.

———. *Husserliana (Hua).* The Hague: Nijhoff, 1950–.

———. *Ideas Pertaining to a Pure Phenomenology and to a Phenomenological Philosophy.* Vol. 2: *Studies in the Phenomenology of Constitution.* Translated by Richard Rojcewicz and André Schuwer. Dordrecht: Kluwer, 1989.

————. *Logical Investigations.* Edited by Dermot Moran. Translated by J. N. Findlay. 2 vols. Vol. 2: *Investigations in Phenomenology and Knowledge.* London: Routledge, 2001.

————. *L'origine de la géométrie.* Translated with an introduction by Jacques Derrida. Paris: Presses Universitaires de France, 1962. [*Edmund Husserl's Origin of Geometry: An Introduction,* by Jacques Derrida. Translated by John P. Leavey. Lincoln: University of Nebraska Press, 1989.]

Jay, Martin. *Downcast Eyes: The Denigration of Vision in Twentieth-Century French Thought.* Berkeley: University of California Press, 1993.

Kant, Immanuel. *Kritik der reine Vernunft.* 1781. Leipzig: Insel Verlag, 1922. [*Critique of Pure Reason.* Translated by Francis Haywood. London: Pickering, 1848.]

————. *Prolegomena zu einer jeden künftigen Metaphysik, die als Wissenschaft wird auftreten können.* 1783. Edited with notes and introduction by Konstantin Pollok. Hamburg: Meiner, 2001. [*Prolegomena to Any Future Metaphysics.* Edited and translated by Gary C. Hatfield. Cambridge: Cambridge University Press, 1997.]

————. *Über Pädagogik.* With an introduction by Jeffrey Stern. Taipei, Taiwan: Thoemmes Press, 1995. Facsimile of the 1803 edition. ["Lectures on Pedagogy." In his *Anthropology, History and Education.* Translated by Mary Gregor et al. Cambridge: Cambridge University Press, 2007.]

Koffka, Kurt. *Principles of Gestalt Psychology.* New York: Harcourt, 1935.

Levinas, Emmanuel. *Totalité et infini: Essai sur l'extériorité.* The Hague: Nijhoff, 1961. [*Totality and Infinity: An Essay on Exteriority.* Translated by Alphonso Lingis. Dordrecht: Kluwer, 1991.]

Malraux, André. *Les voix du silence.* Paris, NRF, 1951. [*The Voices of Silence: Man and His Art.* Translated by Stuart Gilbert. New York: Doubleday, 1953.]

————. *Psychologie de l'art.* Vol. 2: *La creation artistique.* Geneva: Skira, 1949. [*Psychology of Art.* Vol. 2: *The Creative Act.* Translated by Stuart Gilbert. London: Zwemmer, 1949.]

Marcel, Gabriel. *Être et avoir.* New edition with a preface and notes by Jeanne Parain-Vital. Paris: Éditions Universitaires, 1991. [*Being and Having: An Existential Diary.* New York: Harper & Row, 1966.]

Parot, Janine. "À la Sorbonne, Claude Simon part en guerre contre la signification." *Les lettres françaises* 859, January 19–25, 1961.

Pos, H. J. "Phénoménologie et linguistique." *Revue internationale de philosophie* 1 (1939): 354–65. ["Phenomenology and Linguistics." Translated by Robin M. Muller. *Graduate Faculty Philosophy Journal* 31, no. 1 (2010): 35–44.]

Ricoeur, Paul. "La question du sujet: Le défi de la sémiologie." In his *Le conflit des interprétations.* Paris: Seuil, 1969. ["The Question of the Subject: The Challenge of Semiology." In his *The Conflict of Interpretations.* Edited by Don Ihde. Translated by Kathleen McLaughlin. Evanston, Ill.: Northwestern University Press, 1974.]

Sartre, Jean-Paul. *La transcendance de l'ego: Esquisse d'une description phénomé-nologique*. With introduction, notes and appendices by Sylvie Le Bon. Paris: Vrin, 1992. [*The Transcendence of the Ego: An Existentialist Theory of Con-sciousness*. Translated by Forrest Williams and Robert Kirkpatrick. New York: Hill and Wang, 1991.]

———. *L'être et le néant: Essai d'ontologie phénoménologique*. Paris: Gallimard, 1943. [*Being and Nothingness: An Essay on Phenomenological Ontology*. Translated with an introduction by Hazel E. Barnes. New York: Philosophi-cal Library, 1956.]

———. *Qu'est-ce que la littérature?* Paris: Gallimard, 1948. [*What Is Literature?* Translated by Bernard Frechtman. New York: Philosophical Library, n.d. (1949).]

———. "Une idée fondamentale de la phénoménologie de Husserl: L'intentionnalité." *La Nouvelle revue française* (January 1939): 129–31. Repr. in his *Situations I*, 31–35. Paris: Gallimard, 1947. ["A Fundamental Idea of Husserl's Phenomenology: Intentionality." In his *Critical Essays (Situations I)*. Translated by Chris Turner. London: Seagull, 2010.]

Saussure, Ferdinand de. *Cours de linguistique générale*. Edited by Charles Bally and Albert Séchehaye. Critical edition by Tullio de Mauro. Paris: Payot, 2005. [*Course on General Linguistics*. Edited by Charles Bally and Albert Séchehaye. Translated by Wade Baskin. New York: Philosophical Library, 1959].

Spitzer, Leo. "Milieu and Ambiance: An Essay in Historical Semantics." *Philosophy and Phenomenological Research* 3 (September 1942): 1–42.

Taminiaux, Jacques. *Le regard et l'excédent*. The Hague: Nijhoff, 1977.

Uexküll, Jakob von. *Streifzüge durch die Umwelten von Tieren und Menschen— Bedeutungslehre*. Berlin: Verlag von Julius Springer, 1934. [*A Foray into the World of Animals and Humans: With a Theory of Meaning*. Translated by Joseph D. O'Neill. Minneapolis: University of Minnesota Press, 2010.]

Valéry, Paul. *Cahiers*. Edited by J. Robinson-Valéry. 2 vols. Paris: Gallimard, 1973–74. [*Cahiers (= Notebooks)*. Edited by Brian Simpson, Paul Gifford, and Robert Pickering. Translated by Paul Gifford et al. Frankfurt: Peter Lang, 2000–2010.]

Wittgenstein, Ludwig. *Philosophische Untersuchungen*. Frankfurt: Suhrkamp, 1971. [*Philosophical Investigations*. Translated by G. E. M. Anscombe. 3rd ed. New York: Macmillan, 1958.]

Index of names

Index of concepts

literature: 43, 50–51

middle voice (grammar): 95–96
milieu: 20–23
music: 111–12

narcissism (ontological): 91
noncoincidence: 73
norms (social): 99

oblivion: of being, 87; of the sensible,
    88–89; of the subjective, 87
obviousness: 2–7
oculocentrism: 75–76
operative *versus* thematic: 100

painting: 55–56, 60–62, 64
perceptual faith: 4
philosophizing without philosophemes:
    59
potentiality: xi, 24, 37, 47, 59

qualia: 65, 80, 85

realism: 5–6, 18, 99
reduction as leading back: 5

reflexology: 18, 22, 107
reversibility as ultimate truth: 6, 69, 73,
    75, 92

saying and said: 38, 53
seeing anew (*réapprendre à voir*): 3, 9,
    84–85
sensitization: 8, 100–1
sign: arbitrariness of the, 43;
    differentiality of the, 44; material
    indifference of the, 52–53
situation (perceptual): 1–4, 7, 24, 55, 58,
    85, 87, 99
spacing: 26, 46–47, 59, 68, 91
structure: 19–20, 23, 45, 53, 59, 104
style: 50, 63–64, 87

tactility: 73, 75, 114
transcendence: 30–34, 86
transphenomenality: 96–98
turn: expressivist: 13, 40; ontological, 7,
    12–14, 70, 113

untouchable (the): 73–74

virtuality: 24–27, 48

Perspectives in Continental Philosophy
John D. Caputo, series editor

Recent titles:

Emmanuel Alloa, *Resistance of the Sensible World: An Introduction to Merleau-Ponty*. Translated by Jane Marie Todd. Foreword by Renaud Barbaras.

Françoise Dastur, *Questions of Phenomenology: Language, Alterity, Temporality, Finitude*. Translated by Robert Vallier.

Jean-Luc Marion, *Believing in Order to See: On the Rationality of Revelation and the Irrationality of Some Believers*. Translated by Christina M. Gschwandtner.

Adam Y. Wells, ed., *Phenomenologies of Scripture*.

An Yountae, *The Decolonial Abyss: Mysticism and Cosmopolitics from the Ruins*.

Jean Wahl, *Transcendence and the Concrete: Selected Writings*. Edited and with an Introduction by Alan D. Schrift and Ian Alexander Moore.

Colby Dickinson, *Words Fail: Theology, Poetry, and the Challenge of Representation*.

Emmanuel Falque, *The Wedding Feast of the Lamb: Eros, the Body, and the Eucharist*. Translated by George Hughes.

Emmanuel Falque, *Crossing the Rubicon: The Borderlands of Philosophy and Theology*. Translated by Reuben Shank. Introduction by Matthew Farley.

Colby Dickinson and Stéphane Symons (eds.), *Walter Benjamin and Theology*.

Don Ihde, *Husserl's Missing Technologies*.

William S. Allen, *Aesthetics of Negativity: Blanchot, Adorno, and Autonomy*.

Jeremy Biles and Kent L. Brintnall, eds., *Georges Bataille and the Study of Religion*.

Tarek R. Dika and W. Chris Hackett, *Quiet Powers of the Possible: Interviews in Contemporary French Phenomenology*. Foreword by Richard Kearney.

Richard Kearney and Brian Treanor, eds., *Carnal Hermeneutics*.

Aaron T. Looney, *Vladimir Jankélévitch: The Time of Forgiveness*.

Vanessa Lemm, ed., *Nietzsche and the Becoming of Life*.

Edward Baring and Peter E. Gordon, eds., *The Trace of God: Derrida and Religion*.

Jean-Louis Chrétien, *Under the Gaze of the Bible*. Translated by John Marson Dunaway.

Michael Naas, *The End of the World and Other Teachable Moments: Jacques Derrida's Final Seminar*.

Noëlle Vahanian, *The Rebellious No: Variations on a Secular Theology of Language*.

A complete list of titles is available at http://fordhampress.com.